Through Mathematical Eyes

Exploring Relationships in Math and Science

Edited by
Ron Ritchhart

Series Editors
Dennie Palmer Wolf and Julie Craven
with Dana Balick

Heinemann
Portsmouth, NH

Heinemann
A division of Reed Elsevier Inc.
361 Hanover Street
Portsmouth, NH 03801-3912
Offices and agents throughout the world

The author and publisher wish to thank those who have generously
given permission to reprint borrowed material:

Figure 1.1, "Evolution of Women's 100M Freestyle World Record,"
Copyright, USA TODAY. Reprinted with permission.

Chapter 3 figures from EDC: *Human Body Systems*, © 1997 by
Kendall/Hunt Publishing Company. Reprinted by permission of
Kendall/Hunt Publishing Company.

Acquiring editor: Bill Varner
Contributing editor: Maureen Barbieri
Cover illustration: Silvia Cooda
Cover designer: Jenny Jensen Greenleaf
Manufacturing coordinator: Louise Richardson

Library of Congress Cataloging-in-Publication Data

Through mathematical eyes : exploring relationships in math and
   science / edited by Ron Ritchhart.
      p.   cm. — (Moving middle schools)
   ISBN 0-435-07217-X (acid-free paper)
   1. Functions—Study and teaching (Middle school)   I. Ritchhart,
Ron. II. Series.
   QA331.3.T48   1997
511.3'3'0712—dc21   97-5389
                                  CIP

Printed in the United States of America on acid-free paper
01 00 99 98 97   EB   1 2 3 4 5 6

Contents

Acknowledgments

This series, Moving Middle Schools, is the result of many people joining up and buckling down. We want to begin by thanking the author-teachers who were willing to try a venture that was to be a mix of teaching, researching, writing, and collegial exchange. They signed up without a recipe, came to seminars with strangers, taught in unforeseen ways, and wrote after school and into the nights. Right behind them, we want to thank the students who made these projects possible. They, too, were without a blueprint. And they, too, have given generously of their time, their thoughts, and their writing. Behind the teachers are the colleagues and principals who covered classes, read drafts, and made exceptions. Behind those educators are the urban districts that worked with us to endorse serious school reform: Fort Worth, Texas; Pittsburgh, Pennsylvania; Rochester, New York; San Diego and San Francisco, California; and Wilmington, Delaware. Just back of the students are families who stayed up to proofread, trekked to the library one more time, went on field trips, or answered interview questions when they could have gone out, read, napped, or eaten supper.

For this volume, we are enormously grateful to Roy Gould, Donna Foley, and Joan Boykoff Baron for their willingness to bring their wisdom, enthusiasm, and critical perspective to the conversation captured within these pages.

We also owe thanks to another set of "critical friends"—people who worked along with us, even as they asked hard questions and set unforgivingly high standards: Edmund Gordon, Carol Bonilla-Bowman, Melissa Lemons, and Patty Taylor. Most recently, we are indebted to the editors and staff of Heinemann, who were willing to work with us, even though we were, and remain, a collaborative, with all the varied ideas and voices that implies.

Finally, we want to thank those who as many as five years ago were willing to support research on school reform in urban settings. This work grew to become PACE (Performance Assessment Collaboratives for Education), a network of urban school districts committed to high standards of practice for students, teachers, and schools that, historically, have not known sustained support and abundant resources. PACE invented the *Curriculum Seminars* that, in turn, gave birth to this series of books. That original generosity—in particular, the willingness to provide a rare five years of work together—has made us remember that the first meaning of the word *foundation* is that of a solid footing on which a structure can be built. So, we thank Alberta Arthurs, Hugh Price, Jamie Jensen, and Marla Ucelli at the Rockefeller Foundation, and Warren Simmons and Lynn White at the Annie E. Casey Foundation.

Foreword: A Word About This Series

Beginning in 1991, with a grant from the Rockefeller Foundation, PACE, an unusual collaborative of urban educators, got under way. In six sites across the country (Fort Worth, Texas; Pittsburgh, Pennsylvania; Rochester, New York; San Diego and San Francisco, California; and Wilmington, Delaware) teams of teachers began creating "portfolio cultures"—classrooms where growth towards high common standards and reflection was emphasized for both students and teachers. The image of a classroom as a culture where a complex network of daily actions support thinking and imagination provided an important tool for rethinking not just assessment, but curriculum, teaching, and connections to families and the surrounding communities.

It was no accident that this work was centered in middle schools. Early adolescence is one of the most vulnerable—and most promising—moments in the life-span of Americans. Contrary to stereotypic views of adolescents, many students between the ages of ten and fifteen are intensely focused on the world "out there." They want to know "What kind of place is there for me—and others like me?" When the answer is harsh and discouraging, we see cynicism, doubt, and disengagement. When the answer is full and reassuring, we see energy, invention, and insight.

Early in our work on creating portfolio cultures, we began to question the usual proposition that "as soon as schools are orderly, safe, and respectful, we will be able to launch new kinds of learning." Teachers began to wonder aloud, "Couldn't it be that once learning is under way, then we will see orderly, safe, respectful schools?" In the wake of that startling reversal, we began to think about the major learning challenges that young adolescents could take on and enjoy and that could make it possible for many more young people to travel from elementary to high school thinking of themselves as authors, scientists, historians, artists, or mathematicians.

In that process, we developed a unique way of working together that we came to call "curriculum seminars." At the heart of each seminar was a major learning task that is possible and important, but rarely pursued deeply, in middle school. For instance, we imagined middle schools where students graduated able to:

- write powerful nonfiction
- understand concepts like functions that bridge the concrete work of arithmetic with the conceptual world of algebra
- use primary sources to understand lives lived in other times and places

In order to realize that vision, working groups of teachers became involved in a two-year process to develop curriculum that both faced these challenges and made them available to a full range of learners. In the two years that we worked together, teachers, researchers, and outside experts moved through many steps.

- We used portfolios of work from both struggling and accomplished students to investigate what prevents large students from being successful at these key challenges.
- We adopted the role of novice learners in immersions that took us deep into the workrooms and thoughts of adults whose life-work depends on these understandings (journalists, scientists, archaeologists). This took us out into the city to practice journalism; into a collaboration with scientists and mathematicians; and to a museum to look at the artifacts of Mayan civilization.
- We designed and drafted curricula to make these big ideas and powerful strategies available to students.
- We taught those curricula and brought the evidence of student work back to the seminar for help, information, and critique.
- We revised the curricula and taught them again.
- We thought about the resulting student work in the light of demanding performance standards.

This series of books, including *Through Mathematical Eyes*, is the next-to-final phase of this long-term collaboration. In this stage teachers have once again stepped outside of their classrooms, this time to become authors. The chapters here are their reflections on what is possible for young adolescent learners—no matter what their history, their income, their country of origin, or their first language. In this phase we began to reflect in particular on a new vision of accomplished and experienced teachers' work. Whatever the specifics, the teachers who had suddenly become researchers as well as authors insisted that this combination of intense classroom engagement and adult reflection was something they never again wanted to be without.

The last step of this work is now out of our hands. That is the step where other teachers read and reflect and then adapt, implement, and revise once again what they find between these covers so that other students may engage and invent.

Introduction

Learning How to Teach Functions—More than Steps and Techniques

Dennie Palmer Wolf

It is high summer. Classrooms are still sleeping behind pulled shades, the boxes of new books stacked, the floors still scuffed from June, not yet rewaxed. The sky is fog, the air damp, and I've been driven into a secondhand bookstore. There on a low shelf I find treasures: the school books of two and three generations back. I open them and read them as play scripts: the speaking parts and stage directions for recreating how Mr. Watson taught mathematics up on the second floor in the warm autumn of 1927 or how Miss Smith taught health to girls in bloomers. But I also realize that they record the plain, daily steps by which generations of Americans formed their notions of learning, excellence, social studies, and mathematics.

Perhaps my favorite is the 1933–1934 copy of *The Instructor Year-book.*[1] Its owner, Irene Williams, Central School, Parry Sound, has penned her name neatly in the upper right-hand corner of the cover. Inside, a firm check mark indicates each of the articles that Mrs. Williams meant to use. Among them is "Three-step Problems for Sixth Grade" by E. J. Bonner, Principal, City Normal School, Rochester, New York. Opposite a lithograph of an earnest boy in knickers making a bank deposit, ranks of word problems march down the page:

> Thirty-six pupils of a sixth-grade class in the Hawthorne School were each served $\frac{1}{8}$ quart of ice cream costing $1.60 a gallon. What was the total cost of the ice cream?

Tony, the fruit dealer, sells 3 oranges for $.08. How much does he receive for a box containing 18 dozen oranges?

Will's father worked for the Gas and Electric Company for $8.00 a day. He worked 6 days a week for 49 weeks each year. How much did he earn in three years?

We can smile at the oddities: the unbelievably low price of goods, an eight-dollar daily wage, or the stereotypical Tony, the (Italian) fruitseller. More than a half century afterward, in the light of the National Council of Teachers of Mathematics standards, in a year when the results of the Third International Mathematics and Science Study will be announced, in the wake of handheld graphing calculators and chaos theory, we can "tsk" at how routine, even clerical, these "three-step problems" seem.

Enter a middle school mathematics classroom today and you are likely to see students working in small groups; they may well have calculators, and you may even see them leaning over their latest math "investigation." In the name of developing a sense of large numbers, students draw a salary figure from a hat. Then they go to newspapers and magazines and cut out ads for cars, apartments, and groceries they can afford, pasting them into their "budget" journals, and keeping a running total. Or, in the name of geometry, they make the floor plan of a house for which they have to calculate the area of each room as well as the total area. We see students engaged: they chat, compare car prices, run up their square footage with bowling alleys and six-car garages. We notice that each solution is different and that students use outside resources and consult with one another. However, upon close examination, these "investigations" often disappoint.

Yes, data gathering and discussion are alive and well, but fundamentally, Mrs. Williams' mathematics of keeping track remains. Peel back the veneer of many of these "investigations" or "Problems of the Week," and we see the same iterative calculation that students have been doing since third grade. Strip away the "Math Investigation" heading, put away the calculators, and little has changed. The numbers are bigger, the arithmetic is concerned with the total number of square feet rather than the number of oranges, but the basic "shopkeeper arithmetic" remains. We have merely fooled ourselves into believing that by adding the topics of "area" or "budgeting" we have created a mathematics worthy of young adult minds. In essence, calculators and cooperative learning aside, we share the view E. J. Bonner offered Mrs. Williams over a half century ago in *The Instructor Yearbook*: the more steps, the more math.

E. J. Bonner and Mrs. Williams raise other difficult questions as well. If Mrs. Williams' grandson were now a sixth-grade math teacher, his address would not be a "normal" school; instead, he might well be in a contemporary middle school with team-teaching and block scheduling. When his district adopts a new math series, he attends sessions on learning to use geoboards or cooperative learning. When it comes time for him to acquire his professional development credits, he signs up for an after-school series of three sessions on how to do portfolio assessment. Just as with the earlier example of the math investigations, much appears to be different. But is it? Frequently, no. In many cases the fundamental message remains "Here, do this." For his grandmother it was three-step problems; for him it is manipulatives or portfolios. As in training workers on new equipment, the belief is in the tools and techniques, not the operator. Consequently, operating manuals (e.g., teacher's editions) and training sessions (e.g., after-school workshops, summer sessions) are all that is called for. The real work of teaching—deciding what matters in geometry, what images to use to convey a concept, how to diagnose what students understand, how to uproot a serious misconception, how to appraise the success of a lesson—receives little attention. In 1934— and now.

This volume is designed to take issue with all these hard-to-shake beliefs about what constitutes mathematical development for both students and teachers. In the following chapters, mathematics educators show us what can happen when they challenge the premise that more steps is more math; or that adding the topics of budgets and area transforms elementary school arithmetic into middle school mathematics. For teachers grappling with these issues, professional development must become more than merely the gathering of new techniques. It must challenge their assumptions of what constitutes meaningful mathematics.

So what should mathematical education look like? First we need a new image of mathematical learning. Teaching and learning are not well served by the traditional image of a long staircase, ascending through levels of calculation to the high plateau of algebra and then the celestial peak of calculus. Mathematics is a complex enterprise demanding a broad repertoire of skills, strategies, and knowledge. In other words, mathematical learning is not a single steel escalator. It is much more like one of Wittgenstein's territories:[2] It can be entered variously, and traversed differently, the only real requirement is that it should be well mapped. It is possible, though viewed as heretical by some, to teach fundamental algebraic concepts or the basics of mathematical modeling to a student who is still struggling with long division or multiplying fractions. Although those operations are vital, they are not logically or cognitively necessary for understanding such generative notions as variables and functions.

Second, if we want to develop mathematical power in more than a few students, we have to think both ruthlessly and developmentally. We have to ask ourselves, "What are the four or half dozen mathematical ideas that we would be willing to work on continuously throughout middle school, because once students own them, they have the keys to the kingdom?" In this volume, math educators show us what might happen with the courage to seek and invest in a well-chosen generative topic. In the chapters that follow, they demonstrate what it looks like to really work on and develop the concept of functions into a foundation for at least two essential mathematical understandings with long-term payoffs: (1) the ability to model a real-world phenomenon mathematically (to develop "math eyes"), and (2) the capacity to create multiple representations (graphic, linguistic, numerical).

In many respects, this vision could be seen as merely more support for the familiar argument, "less is more." But these educators make a further point: If functions (as well as concepts like probability or rates of change) are so important, then middle school ought to be thought of as one three-year-long laboratory in which students develop a continuously deepening grasp of them. Begin with concrete, linear functions in sixth grade, use seventh grade to push toward models that take in more than one source of variance; by eighth grade expect that these understandings can be used to predict, using the power of formal mathematics. Their message is direct and unforgiving: Cause understanding to happen; don't hope it will unfold.

The third point is that students will never acquire this kind of command of important mathematical ideas if we continue to teach them in splendid isolation. If we want students to understand, rather than merely have acquaintance with concepts like functions, we need collaboration across the usual subject area boundaries. However, this is not a plea for interdisciplinary units with the mathematics shoehorned in. What these educators explore are genuine partnerships: seeking contexts in which building and formalizing a mathematical function will yield insight to both subject areas. For instance, if students want to think about the effects of smoking in biology (as Carrie Wong describes in Chapter 3), they have to collect and graph lung-capacity data from nonsmokers and occasional and heavy smokers, both men and women, and across different ages. In that way students might learn about the complex manner in which smoking affects health, and the power of mathematics to help in investigating and portraying those effects.

But where will such powerful mathematical experiences come from if Mrs. Williams' grandson has little more than the technical training she had? "Teacher training" as we know it is nowhere near nourishing or demanding enough. Instead, the experiences of the teachers suggest quite a different model: the model of curriculum seminars discussed earlier in the foreward to this volume. This book's contributors were all partners, either original or subsequent, in a long-term investigation of the consequences of portfolio assessment. As a part of that investigation, teachers in PACE were regularly involved in two sustained conversations that rarely, if ever, occur where the emphasis is on training teachers in new techniques. In the first conversation about portfolio assessment, teachers spoke—and argued—about what counted as quality in student work. Given that many PACE teachers worked in settings where

Jonathan Kozol's "savage inequalities"[3] once operated, a second conversation erupted. That conversation swirled around the too-often-ignored question, "But what opportunities do students need to have before they can perform to high standards?"

These exchanges proved so habit-forming that we developed a series of national seminars, each focused on a major issue in middle school teaching and learning. This volume resulted from the seminar about designing strong mathematical experiences with generative ideas—especially for students whose opportunities to learn had been limited, interrupted, or challenged. As the seminar evolved, it focused on exploring functions in mathematics and science.

Quite deliberately, the seminar and the exchanges it sparked spread over nearly three years. It began with teachers coming to Harvard's Graduate School of Education for three days of being students: scouring the Museum of Science for evidence of functions, performing experiments, making predictions, collecting data, and graphing findings. (These experiments are discussed in Appendix B.) At that point, teachers went back to their home schools and began to draft units of their own that could help their own students to understand the power of thinking about phenomena, changes, and relationships that could be expressed in mathematical functions. Half a year and much experimentation later, the teachers returned to Boston, each with a possible functions unit in hand, often coupled with at least preliminary samples of students' work. Once again becoming a working seminar, teachers presented and critiqued one another's units, raising hard questions about the power of the assignments to both engage students and instill a lasting command of a powerful mathematical concept. The following fall, based on what they had learned, teachers retaught the unit, sometimes alone, sometimes with colleagues. They collected student work, kept journals, and spoke on the telephone with one another, and with their colleagues at PACE. That work formed the basis for teachers becoming researchers and authors. They reflected on their own and their students' work and began to draft a chapter about their experiences transforming not just the topics but the entire complexion of their middle school mathematics and science classrooms.

The results are reflected in the chapters that follow. The leader of the seminar, Ron Ritchhart, opens by exploring the many ways in which functions surround us and affect our lives. From reading the newspaper to driving to work, Ron shows us that functions have a rich life outside of the math classroom. For those readers unfamiliar with the concept of functions, they will find the examples and simple definitions a useful foundation, showing that the concept can be made available and concrete without losing any of its power. In addressing the question, "What do functions allow us to do?", Ron provides answers that help us see the critical importance of functions in the mathematics curriculum.

In the second chapter, Betsy Berry and Marcy Converse explain how they team taught their seventh graders the core mathematics of functions. Working in a junior high school in rural Maine, they tackle the difficulty of developing students' understanding of mathematics while developing cooperative learning skills and promoting critical thinking. Using open-ended problems and thoughtful discussions, Betsy and Marcy fully exploit the flexibility of their "double periods" of mathematics. Third, Carrie Wong explains how she forged a connection between math and science in her San Francisco seventh grade classroom. Responsible for teacing both math and science, Carrie describes how she used the concept of functions to inform and enliven her teaching of health and human anatomy. In a meaningful inquiry into the effects of smoking, students learn the importance of observation skills, measurement precision, and clear communication.

In the fourth and fifth chapters, Amy Benedicty, Sean Donahoe, and Mike Benway take the math and science connection still further. In chapter four, Amy shows us how a unit on functions gets translated and revised in a new setting. From their shared portable classroom overlooking the city of San Francisco, Sean and Amy weave together math, science, and literature as they explore functions with the seventh graders of Rooftop Alternative School. Amy's transfer across town produces a rich collaboration with Sean, and we see how mathematical work with functions can provide powerful models and tools for understanding relationships in science. In chapter five, Mike Benway pushes headlong into rich scientific inquiry as his students in the after-school Urban Scholars program explore the question, "Do fish sleep?" Working from his perspective as a professional scientist, Mike demonstrates to his students the invaluable nature of functions in exploring and understanding scientific phenomena.

The curriculum seminars have always been about professional dialogue, the kind of rich discussions and serious critique too often missing in our schools, the kind of hot back and forth that stirs both thoughts and emotions. Chapter six provides just such a conversation as a group of critical friends discuss the work of the teachers in the curriculum seminars and the resulting student work. We hope this chapter will help you to better examine and explore the issue of what could and should be expected from middle school mathematicians. Finally, in his conclusion, Ron Ritchhart praises the messy, noisy process of curriculum work that was the heart of the seminars. In exploring the benefits of the process, Ron also recounts what we have learned along the way in terms of both the kind of work teachers need to do and what students need to do in order to develop a rich understanding of functions. Read, join us in this rich professional conversation, and make your own noise as you take these ideas and make them your own.

Notes

1. *The Instructor Yearbook*. 1933. Dansville, NY: F. A. Owen Publishing.
2. Ludwig Wittgenstein (1889–1951) was one of the most influential philosophers of this century. His work focused on uncovering the hidden rules or "grammars" of a discipline or "game" and constructing arguments within that system.
3. Jonathan Kozol has written extensively about the lives of poor and marginalized children in our society. See for example Kozol, J. 1992. *Savage Inequalities*. New York: Harper Collins.

1

Seeing the World Through Mathematical Eyes

Exploring Functional Relationships

Ron Ritchhart

> While with an eye made quiet by the power of harmony, and the deep power of joy, We see into the life of things.
>
> Wordsworth, "Lines Composed a Few Miles Above Tintern Abbey"

There is an ancient folk tale told in India of a wise man and a king. The wise man, having performed many services for the king, is one day called before the court and asked to name his reward. The wise man is committed to a life of austere simplicity, so he graciously declines the king's generous offer of payment and proceeds to respectfully depart the great hall, leaving the king and his guests to commence the chess tournament being prepared by the servants. The king, eager to impress the dignitaries visiting the court and not wanting his guests to think him a miserly and self-centered ruler, summons the wise man back and relentlessly insists on bestowing a bequest upon him. At last, the wise man's resolve appears to soften; his stoic expression gradually transforms into an enigmatic smile. The vast hall grows silent as all the court strains to hear the wise man's request.

In a quiet voice that bespeaks the wise man's complete contentment with life, he makes what the king regards as a rather simple, though somewhat strange, petition. The wise man asks that tomorrow he be given but one grain of rice for the first square of the king's chessboard. The next day, he requests that the amount of rice he is to receive be doubled to two grains, for the second square on the king's chessboard. Each day the amount of rice should be doubled for the next square on the chessboard. And so one grain of rice shall become two grains, and two grains shall become four grains, and so on for each square. With a magnanimous flourish designed to hide his growing self-doubt, the king declares, "Your unorthodox request is most simply granted." And in that instant, the King begins to grow uneasy at the profound powers he has unleashed.

Like many of us, the king in our Indian folk tale let his pride get the better of him. However, it was his blindness to the mathematics of the situation that propelled him heedlessly forward in the fulfillment of an impossible request. The king lacked what we in the PACE curriculum seminars have come to call *mathematical eyes*. While perhaps recognizing that the amount of rice owed was a function of the number of days since the wise man's petition, he lacked the ability to visualize the growth relationship the wise man's request invoked.[1] Consequently, the king's expectation of slow and constant linear growth caused him not to become alarmed when on the 16th day he sent the wise man one pound of rice from the granary. But just a week later it was 128 pounds, and the following week a whopping 8 tons of rice were carried through the streets to the wise man's small house, exposing the full power of exponential growth![2]

Like the king, our mathematical eyes are regularly being tested, though perhaps not in such a dramatic way. Viewing the world from a mathematical perspective does not mean carrying around a pocket calculator or scratch pad on which to perform an endless series of calculations. Rather, it entails having a sense of quantities, an appreciation of and sensitivity to connections and interdependencies, a notion of functional or cause-and-effect relationships, and the ability to construct visual images to capture these relationships.

A quick glance through the newspaper provides a vast array of stories whose meaning can only be grasped with an understanding of mathematical relationships and an ability to see how one event is a function of another. *The Wall Street Journal* (Figure 1–1) reports

FIGURE 1-1.

the third largest one-day drop ever in the DOW Jones industrial average following the release of information indicating the good news that unemployment is at a new low.[3] Readers are left to sort out the relationship between unemployment, interest rates, stock prices, and bond prices. The *Boston Globe* (Figure 1–1) reports that due to record snows in 1996, Logan International Airport stands to make a killing on its snow insurance policy, which pays $50,000 for every inch of snow over 44 inches.[4] The article reports that the policy cost the authorities $400,000 and the average Boston snowfall is 42.7 inches, leaving readers to make sense of the gamble both the insurance company and the airport authorities took.

USA Today (Figure 1–1) recounts the gains elite women athletes have made in championship track and field events, reporting that over the past decade women's record-breaking speeds have improved at a rate of 14 meters a minute while men have improved only half as much.[5] The mental construction of a graph comparing the improvement rate of men and women over time allows the reader to play with a variety of future scenarios and critically examine the claim that women may outpace men over the next 50 to 60 years. In the sports section, a separate table (Figure 1–2) reports the declining times for the women's 100-meter freestyle over the years without any accompanying interpretation. Presented with these raw data, the reader must construct his or her own understanding of the rate of change.

An Australian advertisement (Figure 1–3) presents a graphical representation of inflation, showing that not all consumer goods are affected equally. The unique area model representation of the data provides the reader with an intuitive grasp of rates of change while at the same time making it difficult to directly compare the increases for individual products. Furthermore, the reader is left wondering about classes of products: has the rate of growth been greater for food staples or for energy?

As these examples attest, our world abounds with quantitative information, relationships, and connections. To truly see into the life of things we must develop many perspectives from which to view the world, including a mathematical one. As Ellen Langer notes in *Mindfulness*: "If Archimedes had had his mind set only on taking a bath, he probably would not have discovered the displacement of water."[6] The rest of this chapter will explore how the mathematical perspective, our "mathematical

FIGURE 1–2.

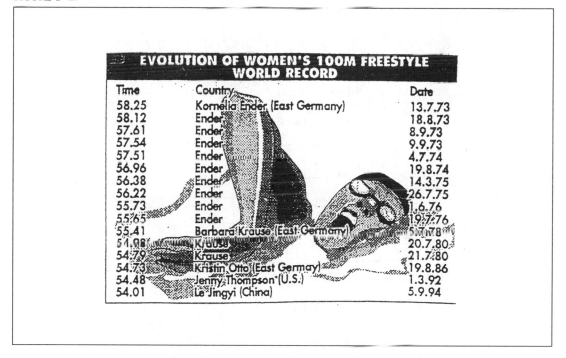

EVOLUTION OF WOMEN'S 100M FREESTYLE WORLD RECORD		
Time	Country	Date
58.25	Kornelia Ender (East Germany)	13.7.73
58.12	Ender	18.8.73
57.61	Ender	8.9.73
57.54	Ender	9.9.73
57.51	Ender	4.7.74
56.96	Ender	19.8.74
56.38	Ender	14.3.75
56.22	Ender	26.7.75
55.73	Ender	1.6.76
55.65	Ender	19.7.76
55.41	Barbara Krause (East Germany)	5.7.78
54.98	Krause	20.7.80
54.79	Krause	21.7.80
54.73	Kristin Otto (East Germay)	19.8.86
54.48	Jenny Thompson (U.S.)	1.3.92
54.01	Le Jingyi (China)	5.9.94

eyes" is enhanced by an understanding of where functions exist in our lives, what functions are, and how they open up new avenues of inquiry and facilitate greater understanding of the world around us.

This examination of the fertile mathematical world of functions will expose the topic of functions as an elegant container for the coming together of an abundance of mathematical ideas, including rates, ratios, variables, graphing, algebra, data collection, computation, statistics, fractions, and technology. In the midst of this expansive content run four important themes that make functions not just a generative topic, but a powerful, central, and unifying idea in mathematics: modeling phenomena, predicting outcomes, understanding variability, and communicating mathematically.

FIGURE 1–3.

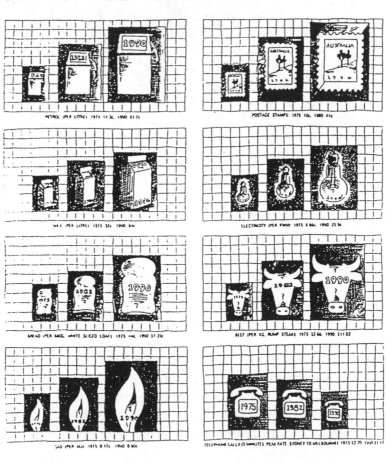

What Are Functions Anyway?

Looking at Relationships in Our Daily Lives

It is 7:15 A.M. and the alarm sounds for the third time. You roll over and look at the clock, trying to make out the exact position of the minute and hour hands. You do not stop to think that the correspondence between the revolving of the earth on its axis in relationship to the sun and the position of the second, minute, and hour hands represents a functional relationship, a special one-to-one correspondence between the exact position of the planet in space and the spatial placement of the plastic hands on your bedside clock. But where would you be if this fundamental relationship had not been understood and reproduced? Snug in bed and late for work, no doubt! Last night, when you set your alarm, you marked a special point in this correspondence, the time you wanted to arise. However, when the alarm rang and alerted you to this moment, you rolled over and pushed the snooze button, being well aware of the relationship between the number of times the snooze button is pressed and the amount of additional slumber time you will be awarded.

As you finally stumble out of bed toward the shower, you encounter a host of relationships that you have completely internalized. Adeptly you adjust the flow of hot and cold water, knowing that achieving the correct correspondence between hot and cold is crucial to obtaining the perfect temperature for your shower. You have set the shower knobs exactly one and a third turns for hot and three fourths for cold, to achieve not only the perfect temperature but the exact water pressure you enjoy. As you shower, you remember your water bill sitting unpaid on the kitchen counter, reminding you that the amount of water used is a function of your time in the shower.

And so the day progresses through a series of relationships that you have internalized: the darkness of your toast as a function of the setting on the toaster, the doneness of your egg as a function of its boiling time, your choice of overcoats as a function of the temperature, your commute time as a function of the number of cars on the road. To say that these relationships are internalized does not mean you are not aware of them. In fact, your performance depends on your being aware of them in both an intuitive and mathematical sense. This does not mean that you draw graphs, compute ratios, or develop formulas around these everyday functions. Rather, you sense them and make quantitative adjustments, such as lengthening the cooking time of your egg, turning the toaster knob another 15 degrees, or adjusting your estimated time of arrival at work based on the heaviness of the traffic.

Functions Long Ago and Far Away

Now imagine waking up not to the sound of your alarm clock, but to the clanging bells in the church tower at the University of Pisa in 1585. You are Galileo Galilei. You get dressed and leave your room for your morning prayers. As you traverse the length of the chapel, you pay little attention to the caretaker performing the daily ritual of lighting the lamps in the chandeliers; immersed as you are in your studies and thoughts of the moment. However, in this meditative place your steps slow and you watch, at first distractedly and then with growing fascination, as the worker releases the chandelier and the lamp swings across the room. For a moment, you are mesmerized watching the lamp swing back and forth, and then you begin to notice a regularity to the lamp's swing. When it was first released, the lamp moved in a wide arc across the width of the chapel. Gradually, the length of the arc diminishes, but it seems to be taking the same amount of time for the chandelier to swing across the room. The time appears independent of the length of the arc.

The caretaker lights and releases a second chandelier at the front of the chapel near the altar. It hangs from a shorter chain and, when released, seems to swing back and forth more quickly than the first. Using your own heartbeat to measure the time, you begin to test your hypothesis that the period of the swing is independent of the length of the arc. As the caretaker continues about his business, you are sure you have made an important discovery. Excitedly, you race back to your room. For you realize that the chandelier is a pendulum whose behavior can be described using the new mathematical tools you have been learning at the university. Whereas previously you have only been able to count and quantify, the concept of variables present in the newly introduced Hindu-Arabic system allows you to express relationships—in essence, to create a function.[7]

After extensive data collection and mathematical analysis, you are able to publish an important mathematical discovery. Using the mathematics made possible by the presence of variables, you share with your colleagues your *Law of the Pendulum*, in which you state that the period of a pendulum's swing is independent of the arc of its swing and that the period of the swing is dependent only on the length of pendulum. When the length of a pendulum is quadrupled, the time it takes to swing back and forth doubles. When the length is increased nine times, the time is tripled. And so you are able to conclude that for the ratio of any two pendulum lengths, l, the ratio of their periods p is equal to the $\sqrt{l}$ or $p = \sqrt{l}$. The time of the period for an individual pendulum, t, can be obtained by taking the square root of the length of the pendulum as measured in feet, f, and multiplying by $1.\overline{1}$ or $t = \sqrt{f} \cdot 1.\overline{1}$.

When Is It a Function?

Our world abounds in both unnoticed and implicit relationships, as these two early morning anecdotes attest. However, it is only when we recognize and explicitly identify and represent these relationships that we call them *functions*. A "mathematical" function represents the establishment of a clear and specific connection between the two variables of the relationship that can be expressed quantitatively as either a rule/formula, a table of values, or a graph. We then let this quantitative expression stand for or represent the abstract functional relationship in much the same way as we let numerals represent the abstract notion of a number. For consistency and clarity, we often use the rule/formula as a shorthand to name or refer to a specific function as a mathematical object.

What Do Functions Allow Us to Do?

Functions allow us to see the power of mathematics much the way Galileo did when he expressed the need for a mathematics to describe and model the phenomenon he was observing. They allow us to move from the specific case to the general by changing our focus from representing quantities to representing relationships. Using our understanding of functions to construct models, we are able to develop an understanding of the change and variation expressed by variables, make predictions about outcomes, and learn to communicate and represent mathematical information.

Construct Models

Functions shift our emphasis from numerical quantities to relationships. Our environment is certainly rich with quantitative information that provides ample need and opportunity for counting, measuring, and computation, yet the arithmetic of quantities only permits us to model static situations in which all of the information is present. We count how many cans of soda in one case and combine it with the number of cans in a second case to find out how many cans of soda in two cases. However, functions allow us to examine relationships and model variable situations in which the information changes but the relationship stays the same. If we know that there are 12 cans of soda to a case, we are able to determine the total number of sodas (t) in any number of cases (c): $t = 12c$. Furthermore, performing operations on a basic function (functions of functions) allows us to model dynamic situations where the relationship is not stable but changes over time, such as in the case of weather patterns or the population of trout in a specific lake over time. Thus, we can examine the cumulative effects of changes in various parameters associated with a function whose core base is itself always changing.

This shift in emphasis from quantities to relationships allows us to make predictions, test hypotheses, display and communicate trends and relationships, and explore different scenarios. Only through a focus on relationships can we develop any real mathematical understanding of the world and its possibilities. What we can understand about ourselves or the world in which we live through counting and measuring is limited. Constructing models of events allows us to understand them better, anticipate outcomes, and consider possibilities.

Understand Variables

Most students first encounter variables as unknowns when they are asked to solve for x in a beginning algebra class. In such situations, the variable represents a specific quantity that can be determined through a series of algebraic manipulations. Although this is certainly a legitimate role for variables, it is an impoverished one. In solving for unknowns, students do not have a chance to encounter the "variable" or changing nature of x. It is in the representation of this variability that the true power of variables lies. Functions expose this variability and make it particularly salient. With functions, the single case of x is not as important as all cases of x. What happens to the output, y, as x changes over time? How are all x's and y's related?

Understanding and employing variables in this way, not as unknowns but as representing all possibilities, students can formulate generalizations or construct models of the relationships they encounter. These formulations allow them to interpret, make sense of, and manipulate factors related to change in a connected and holistic manner. Combined, the use of variables and the notion of dependency relationships allow us to tie together a string of similar, repeated operations into a unified whole called a function. For example, while the use of variables allows us to express the relationship between area and the length and width of a rectangle, an understanding of the functional relationship provides us with an intuitive sense of what happens to the area of a room as one or both dimensions are changed. Without this relational understanding, we would need to recompute every instance of change in which we are interested without any sense of connection between one computation and the next. Functions allow us to chunk this information together and recall it as a whole rather than as discrete parts or operations. They enable us to "see into" formulas and to understand in general terms the effects of factors such as compound interest, cooking times and temperatures, wind-chill factors, and miles per hour.

Make Predictions

Using functions to model relationships allows us to achieve a new level of predictive ability. We can make predictions about hypothetical events and about general outcomes rather than specific quantities. Thus, predictions associated with functions are different from those connected to estimation. Estimation is the type of prediction attached to quantitative situations; it answers the question "about how many?" Even probability provides an estimate of about how many times something is likely to happen. Estimation's main purpose is to save us time in counting or completing complicated computations. Good estimation skills require a feel for the quantities with which we come in contact.

By comparison, the predictions associated with functions modeling natural phenomena ask the question "what can we expect to happen under these circumstances?" These predictions draw on our understanding of relationships and enable us to consider the outcome of various possibilities and scenarios. Depending on the type of situation we are modeling, we can predict the outcome with varying degrees of accuracy. We can predict exactly the amount of tax for any dollar purchase and the cost of our auto insurance (if we know the insurance company's formula), but we may only be able to roughly predict the amount of time it will take for all 38,000 runners of the Boston marathon to walk across the starting line. The quality of our predictions is directly linked to the specificity of our models. When we can identify, measure, and incorporate every relevant variable into our model, we can predict with amazing accuracy. When our information is partial, the models we construct will be incomplete and the predictions rough.

Communicate Mathematical Information

Functions are a type of shorthand. A function in math and science expresses a dependency relationship in which one factor, variable, or outcome is dependent on one or more other factors or variables.[8] Functions are usually expressed as rules or formulas, but the relationship can also be shown through a table of values, described qualitatively, or presented as a graph. Embedded in each of these representations is the pairing of values such that each set of inputs has exactly one output. However, the representation itself is not the function; the dependency relationship, or pairing of values, is the function.

Different representations of functions are desirable in different situations to best communicate the mathematical information that the function conveys. As far back as 2000 B.C., the Babylonians used tables of values for finding reciprocals, squares, and square roots.[9] Today we still find the use of tables of values an important and meaningful way to represent functions. We regularly make use of tables in figuring sales tax, postal rates, and our "ideal" weights. During the Middle Ages, notions of dependency relationships between quantities were expressed as *verbal descriptions*. Description still represents perhaps the most common, though least mathematically formal, way we make use of functions in our daily life, as when a child describes the growth of a puppy, a teenager describes a parent's anger as he or she turns up the stereo, or we describe our progress on a task over time. Descartes' invention of the coordinate plane in the seventeenth century provided a fourth way of representing functions. The graph of a functional relationship can capture in a compact and concise manner the variable nature of the relationship, the descriptive nature of its dependency relationship, and the quantitative values associated with that relationship.

Conclusion

Functions are a rich and multifaceted topic. They have been described variously as the central theme uniting the study of algebra, the very soul of mathematics, and a necessary component for any "real appreciation of mathematics."[10] Functions are important because they move our thinking from a focus on the quantitative characteristics of things (how much? how many?) to the examination of relationships. This shift in thinking gives us the power to model relationships and explore connections that allow us *to see into the life of things*. The construction of appropriate models gives us new powers of prediction, allowing us to examine "what if" scenarios and determine outcomes for events that have only been imagined. This predictive ability of models provides us with a valuable decision-making tool. If only the Indian king in our folk tale had had this understanding, he would not have had to empty his granaries to discover the effects of exponential growth.

In working with functions, students gain access to the power of algebra and learn how to model variability and change. Only through work with functions do students confront the true meaning and implications of variables. As students develop mathematical eyes with which to see the world, they must also develop the tools to communicate in this new world. Working back and forth between the various representations of functions gives students the opportunity to master a powerful set of tools for communicating mathematical information. In doing so, they achieve a new level of mathematical literacy.

Notes

1. The amount of rice the wise man is to receive is a function of the days since the request. The growth of the rice follows an exponential function because the quantity of rice changes by a constant factor of 2. The day of the request or the square of the chessboard is used to determine how many times the rice has doubled. On the second day the rice has doubled once. On the third day the rice has doubled twice. Therefore, the day −1 can be used to tell us how many times to double the rice. Since the rice is doubling, we use 2 as a base and raise it to the power of *days − 1*. For any day then, the amount of rice can be determined by $2^{(days-1)}$. In the story, the rice R is a function of the number of days d. If N is that function, then $R = N(d) = 2^{(d-1)}$. Exponential functions are special because of their ever-accelerating rate of growth.

2. As you can imagine, counting grains of rice is a laborious and time-consuming process for anyone, even a mathematician. On the 12th day there were $2^{(12-1)}$ or 2,048 grains of rice, weighing approximately one ounce (check it out yourself!). Consequently, we are able to move from counting the rice to merely weighing it. Nonetheless, on the 64th day we are still left to weigh out approximately 140, 737,488,400 tons of rice!

3. Dave Kansas, "Was the 171-Point Drop a Blip or a Bear?" *Wall Street Journal*, March 11, 1996, p. C1.

4. Matthew Berlis, "Wager on Airport Amount Insures $2m Pay-off for State," *Boston Globe*, March 9, 1996, p. 14.

5. "Women Gain Ground on Men in Sport," *USA Today*. Tim Friend and Anita Manning, January 2, 1992, p. D1.

6. Ellen Langer. 1989. *Mindfulness*, p. 118. Reading, Mass.: Addison-Wesley.

7. The actual term "function" was not used until a century later, in 1694, by Leibniz and Bernoulli. Euler developed the notation to express functions a century after that.

8. The mathematician Dirichlet showed that this was not always the case. His so-called salt and pepper function, which pairs every rational number with 0 and every irrational number with 1, shows that functions can be arbitrary and lack regularity. Nonetheless, mathematicians and scientist generally find such functions uninteresting for study.

9. This synthesis of the history of functions is drawn from the work of Cooney and Wilson, "Teachers Thinking About Functions: Historical and Research Perspectives," pp. 131–158 and T. Tomberg, T. Carpenter, and E. Fennema, "Toward a Common Research Perspective," pp. 1–9. Both articles appear in T. Romberg, E. Fennema, and T. Carpenter, eds., *Integrating Research on the Graphical Representations of Functions*, 1993, Hillsdale, N.J.: Erlbaum.

10. See Cooney and Wilson (Ibid., p. 137) for a discussion of these historical comments made by Breslich in 1928 and by Klein in 1904.

2

Making Functions Meaningful

The Mount View Story

Betsy Berry and Marcy Converse

It was January 2. The "challenge" was posted on chart paper on the wall of Marcy Converse's seventh grade mathematics classroom at Mount View Junior High.

Draft . . . Draft . . . Draft . . .
Children's Book Challenge
For the past few weeks, you have been studying about mathematical patterns and functions. Your challenge is to share this new knowledge by producing a children's book that features the concept of functions.

You will be working in small groups selected by your teacher. Each person in the group will contribute to the creation of the book and will also be individually responsible for communicating their understanding of functions. Research for the book will involve conducting an experiment or exploration, collecting data, and making graphs. A group presentation of your book will also be required.

Our unit on functions was just beginning, but it was our intent to give the students an idea of what they would be expected to do as a culminating activity. We told them that they would receive a final copy of that challenge later in the month. We hoped that by setting the stage for this project, we might create a "need to know" among the students. To some extent, our hopes were realized when the first question asked in each of Marcy's four classes was "What is a function?"

In the fall of 1995, when Ron Ritchhart initially invited us to be a part of the functions project, this was one of the first issues we as teachers had to confront. Just what are functions? Why are they important? And how do we make them meaningful to our seventh graders? Marcy and I had teamed up last year to teach a similar unit, in response to a move in the junior high to longer class periods and heterogeneous grouping. Marcy had expressed a desire to move away from traditional skills-based instruction and find a way to be more responsive to the needs and interests of her students. As a math facilitator for Maine's Statewide Systemic Initiative, I had jumped at the opportunity to team-teach with her for the year and spend time back in the classroom with students as a balance to my administrative duties.

So Marcy and I accepted Ron's invitation. We were excited to have an opportunity to team-teach once again and to revisit the work on patterns and functions that we had begun the previous year. To allow us time to work together in her classroom, Marcy negotiated with her colleagues on her seventh grade team for a new class schedule for a one-month period beginning immediately after Christmas break. This permitted her to meet with each of her four classes every other day for 105 minutes. This schedule made it possible for me to arrange my work schedule so that we could be together for one full class period every other day. It also gave us a 55-minute preparation period each day before Marcy's teaching schedule started, providing a wonderful opportunity for collaboration.

Our schedule set, the next step was to revisit what we had already done. As we began to discuss the previous year's unit, I remembered how I had struggled for many years as a high school teacher to help students understand and make sense of the concept of functions. Marcy and I talked about how we had learned about functions ourselves in our high school algebra or precalculus courses and how little meaning that had for us. We remembered that the starting point for learning about functions, both as students and as teachers, seemed to have been with the definition: A function is a set of ordered pairs (x,y), such that for any x, there is one and only one y. How was that going to have meaning to our kids? We then talked about what had gone well with the unit we had taught together the previous year, and what needed improvement. We had designed lessons that focused on using manipulatives to create and discover patterns and creating tables and graphs from those patterns. We had introduced writing mathematical rules and equations using variables. All of these class activities had been accessible to all our students. That was an important criterion that we wanted to keep in mind as we planned our new functions unit.

We had previously included experimentation as part of the students' experiences, but we agreed that we had not succeeded in connecting the data collection and graphing of the experiments to the manipulative activities that led to the creation of tables and rules. We also felt that we had not adequately articulated the goals and outcomes of the lessons for the students. Perhaps we had been more concerned with covering the topic than with effectively nurturing the understanding of our students.

As we talked and reviewed what we had done the previous year and considered the possibilities for our new unit, we focused on the need to create experiences that allowed students to identify dependency relationships between two values, to discover patterns and express them as rules of correspondence, and to connect various representations of functions in order to facilitate their development of both a "process" and an "entity" perspective of functions. (These perspectives are discussed more fully in Chapter 7.) We also wanted to design lessons that would challenge and engage our best students but still remain accessible for the others.

We added a new twist to our unit this year. To help us focus on our students' progress, and evaluate our effectiveness at providing good lessons to facilitate that progress, we selected four representative students, two boys and two girls, to observe more closely in class. We would use their work to help us assess our progress as teachers and guide our future decisions about our curriculum. Two of these students were also interviewed by Ron when he visited in the middle of the unit, and three were interviewed by the science facilitator very near the end of the unit as another means of gauging our progress as teachers.

The four students we chose to focus on were all quite different, representing the range of students in the classroom. The first was Natalie, a bright and motivated student. She is a logical thinker and an adept problem solver who enjoys a challenge. She participates frequently in whole-class discussions and takes a leadership role when working in a group. As a top student in all subjects, Natalie is always well prepared and expresses herself well verbally and in writing. We knew that she would let us know when she was challenged or bored or in need of more instruction.

The second student, Laramie, is a careful and conscientious student who at the beginning of the school year seemed bothered by open-ended problems and was afraid to risk a wrong approach or answer. He was gradually becoming more of a risk taker, gaining confidence in his problem-solving abilities as the year progressed. We wanted to monitor Laramie's reaction to the open-ended tasks that we planned to use throughout the unit.

Zeben was our third student, enthusiastic and energetic. A tactile and visual learner, Zeben is right in the middle of any hands-on group activity. Although he participates frequently in class discussions, he can be impulsive and quick to draw conclusions. He lacks the follow-through that could make him a more successful student. His homework is rarely completed, writing is a struggle, and his achievement in all his classes is average to below average. Little feedback comes from his household in spite of his frequent minor behavior problems and low academic grades. We knew Zeben would be engaged in the functions unit, but we wanted to monitor his ability to analyze the data and make the connections that learning about functions requires.

Finally, there was Sari, a shy student, who only occasionally participated in class discussions. She does not often take an active physical role in hands-on group activities, but prefers instead to be a listener and a recorder. Although she is not openly curious or enthusiastic about class activities, Sari follows directions well, stays on task, and is always well prepared for class. We wanted to make sure that our unit really developed an understanding of functions and not just a set of surface skills. Our observations of Sari would help us gauge how effective our tasks were in building understanding.

Throughout the unit, our focus on these four students provided us with valuable information to guide our teaching. For example, midway through the unit, Natalie wrote on a student self-assessment form: "I'm still not very sure about [representing patterns with] variables and expressions. I have a harder time than normal, but I'm starting to get the hang of it." We took this as our cue to include an additional activity that would give all the students more experience with these concepts (the U-Say, I-Say lesson, which will be explained later).

Our intense focus on these four students also showed us that our perceptions of students can be misleading. When we observed Zeben and Sari during class activities and later, more carefully, on videotapes, we were pleased to see Sari taking the lead in her group and actively engaging in the lessons by giving instructions and measuring and collecting data herself. We caught Zeben thinking and questioning as he investigated the ball-bounce and the pendulum problems with his group. Throughout the unit the progress of these four students reassured us that we were having some success at engaging and involving diverse learners.

Four questions guided us in planning the unit: "What are our outcomes for the unit? What is it we want students to understand? What will understanding look like? How can we get students to exhibit their knowledge in multiple ways?" We wanted our students to develop an intuitive understanding of functions. We wanted to help them see the world with mathematical eyes. We wanted them to see the connections among data tables, graphs, symbolic rules, and verbal descriptions and to realize that *all* are ways to represent functions. We also wanted them to understand dependency relationships. We did not expect students to be able to create a sophisticated definition of a function. We did expect them to look for patterns in explorations, experiments, tables, and graphs and to attempt to describe those patterns in words and symbolic sentences.

To help us organize our work and to give our students a specific set of outcomes to refer to throughout the unit, we settled on the performance descriptions from the consultation draft of the *New Standards for Middle Schools.*[1] We created a classroom poster that read:

Students will:
- discover, describe, and generalize patterns, including linear, exponential, and simple quadratic relationships, and represent them with variables and expressions
- represent relationships with tables, graphs in the coordinate plane, and verbal and/or symbolic rules
- analyze tables, graphs, and rules to determine functional relationships
- find solutions for unknown quantities in linear equations and in simple equations and inequalities

This poster helped our students answer for themselves: "What is it that I need to know and be able to do in this unit?" As we debriefed the class after each activity we asked them to think about which items on the poster were evident in the lesson. We felt that this helped students articulate their understanding as they responded to self-assessment questions that we posed to them at various times throughout the unit.

When he met with us in the fall, Ron had shared some of the work that other teachers in the project were doing. We especially liked Amy Benedicty's children's stories idea and decided to adapt it to our unit in the form of the "children's book challenge." We wanted to use this challenge for several reasons. We wanted to create a "need to know" and to give students a reason for their work. We also hoped it would be a piece of our assessment of their individual and group progress and understanding as well as an assessment of the success of our unit. It also enabled us to meet the needs of students who have a difficult time with "traditional" written work but still may be acquiring some understanding of the mathematics.

Before beginning we knew that Zeben was just such a student. Indeed, he served as an excellent representative of others like him throughout the unit. In the class activities we could "see" him learning, but it was difficult to detect that learning in the written work he produced. Midway through the unit we gave students a writing assignment in which we asked them: "Think about the unit on functions that we have been working on. What do you know about functions? Tell as much as you can. What do you not understand?" We got a very brief and direct response from Zeben, "I don't know that much about functions, because I really do not get it yet." However, our observations of his behavior in class implied that a lot of learning was taking place. He easily questioned the results his group got on the ball-bounce problem and suggested alternative strategies for collecting data. But, because he struggles when it comes time to put things down on paper and we struggle at evaluating other, more active evidence of learning, it was difficult to document his progress. Zeben helped us come back to this concern many times during the unit. It is not an issue we have resolved. We continue to struggle with how much students' communication of understanding depends on their ability to express that understanding in writing.

As we were planning our unit together, Marcy raised an additional concern about her seventh-grade group as a whole. She described them as less self-directed and responsible than the previous year's class. This was demonstrated in a variety of ways. They had difficulty working effectively in groups. They were much more negligent about completing homework, and they paid little attention to her "warm-up" problems and directions that we posted on the overhead projector at the beginning of each class. Previous classes had responded easily to the overhead instructions, sometimes coming into the room during their preceding break to sneak a peek at the overhead so that they could begin work. This class tended to ignore whatever was on the screen until it was brought to their attention.

For this reason we included as part of our initial work during this unit the creation of a "Collaborative Learning Community Contract." During the summer of 1994, both Marcy and I had participated in a Critical Skills Institute through Antioch New England Graduate School. The Critical Skills Classroom is a dynamic, comprehensive model for experiential learning. It is driven by desired outcomes and characterized by progressive cycles of problem-based challenges for students working as a collaborative learning community. We felt we were becoming experienced at designing problems and challenges that had the potential for engaging our students, but we needed to strengthen our community-building skills and help our students improve their cooperation and collaboration skills. When we first presented the "Children's Book Challenge" to our students, we had asked them what they needed to know or be able to do. One of the first things that they volunteered, in addition to asking "What is a function?," was "We'll need to be able to work together." Marcy spent some time with each class brainstorming what that meant and helping them to create and commit to a set of standards for behavior and attitudes for their time in class. After it was completed, all members of the class were asked to select the one or two items on the list that they thought were most important for them to work on and to sign the contract demonstrating their commitment to do that.

Collaborative Learning Community
Block 2
We, the individuals of Block 2 Math Class, hereby agree to strive for the following behaviors and attitudes in order to help create a positive and successful Collaborative Learning Community.

- Give ideas
- Participate—be involved
- Help others
- Listen to others
- Be enthusiastic
- Have fun
- Stay on task
- Give positive feedback, not criticism
- Be open to new ideas
- Be willing to work with other people
- Have good communication and teamwork

Our signatures indicate that we will try our best to model the above behaviors.

Our plan for the unit provided for a variety of activities, lessons, problems, and experiences that would address the first three outcomes on the classroom poster. We were trying to use problems that would build on our students' experiences from their previous mathematics classes. It was also important to use a variety of materials and to feature explorations that might lead easily to the detection of patterns and the formulation of algebraic expressions. This would help students understand the *process* of putting a function together. We also planned to include experiments that would demonstrate the fuzzy nature of practicing real mathematics while giving our students practice and opportunity to look at the world with mathematicians' eyes. We settled on "The Grange Hall Problem," "The Bottle Function," and "The Ball-Bounce Problem" for our preliminary plans. "The Tile Layer's Problem" and "Pages in a Book" were assigned as homework.

The Grange Hall Problem was the first activity in our unit. We chose it because it generates a simple linear function that students might generalize by manipulating and analyzing the materials or by examining the values in their data table. It is our version of pattern block trains adapted from a volume in *Patterns and Functions* the NCTM Addenda Series.[2] We began the lesson by describing the following scenario aloud to our students:

> You and the other members of your group run a catering company. You have often been responsible for planning and setting up for wedding receptions around the area in Elks' clubs, Legion halls, and Grange halls. You have a wedding reception to plan that is being held in a remote part of Monroe, Maine. The mother of the bride is very particular and requires that the tables be set up in one long continuous and connected banquet table. When you finally find the Grange hall where the reception is to be held, you notice that there are only triangular tables in the storage closet. Only one person can sit at each edge of one of the tables. You are uncertain how many people will be attending, but

you want to be ready. Investigate the problem by determining the number of people for one table, two tables, three tables, etc., and record your information in a data table. How many people could you seat at a banquet with 20 tables? 50 tables? 99 tables? Is there a pattern? Be prepared to share your data and a description of your pattern in words.

We checked to see if every group had people who felt they understood the problem and asked them to talk as a group about what the problem was about. We then asked for any clarifying questions and modeled the building of the table chain with pattern blocks on the overhead projector. We also modeled a T-chart to collect the data for the number of tables and corresponding number of people who could be seated. There were boxes of pattern blocks for each group.

The students worked in six groups of four. They seemed eager and immediately went to work. They used pattern blocks to build their banquet tables, counting the possible seats and recording the information. The blocks were used in every group, but not necessarily by every student. Some students watched a neighbor build and some seemed able to construct and collect data from a mental image of the problem. After a few minutes we could see that most groups had collected 6 or 8 data pairs and some had begun to predict the value for 20 tables. It seemed evident that some students could see and continue the pattern, although they had not yet begun to articulate the pattern.

We asked them to pause in their group discussions and allow us to collect their results in a class data table. We called on each group in turn and collected pairs of numbers that we recorded on a data chart on the overhead projector (Figure 2–1). When students disagreed, as in the case of 20 tables, we wrote down both responses and had the class check their results.

We then asked students to describe in their own words the patterns they saw in their models or the tables of values. Some samples of their descriptions:

FIGURE 2–1.

Table	Number of People
1	3
2	4
5	7
10	12
13	15
20	22 (24)
107	109
1,000,000	1,000,002
t	

"There is one seat for each table on the sides of the banquet chain and one seat on each end."

"For every table, two more seats are added."

"There are three seats on each table, but you lose two seats at the places where the tables are joined."

"The numbers in the table just increase by two."

Next, we wanted to see if students could connect a symbolic expression to their verbal expression. They had had some experience with the use of variables in writing and solving puzzle problems earlier in the year, but we were uncertain of their ability to transfer this knowledge; for that matter, we were uncertain what experience with using symbols to describe patterns they may have had in earlier grades. We asked the students to create a symbolic sentence using P to represent the number of people and t to represent the number of tables. Most groups were able to express the relationship as $P = t+2$. As we neared the end of the class period, we talked briefly about how the number of people that we could seat was dependent on the number of tables in the chain, that P is a function of t. We introduced dependent and independent variables and functional notation for the first time: $P = f(t) = t+2$. As usual we were rushed for time at the end of the period, but we hoped to lay the groundwork for building vocabulary and beginning to build the understanding necessary to identify dependence relationships and to express rules of correspondence.

We then introduced their homework, the Tile Layer's Problem:

> You are an employee of the Taylor Tile Company.
>
> Your job is to lay tile flooring. Your boss has asked you to figure out a problem for him. He would like to know a quick way to determine how many tiles are needed along the border of any square tiled floor a customer might request. He is looking for a general rule he can use to figure out how many tiles are necessary to create the border. It is your task to find this rule.
>
> In order to solve this special problem, you need to collect information from at least 8 different-sized floors. Use the graph paper provided to represent your square tiled floors. Collect your data in an organized way. Explore any patterns you see. Be prepared to discuss your information and observations.

We hoped this task would reinforce the key aspects of the Grange Hall Problem: investigating a problem, creating a data table, looking for a pattern, and creating a symbolic generalization of a function. When we met again, we faced our perennial problem. Nearly half of the class, including Zeben, couldn't find or had not completed the problem, inhibiting the discussions in their groups. We overcame this obstacle by having those in each group who had completed their work report to those who had not, then the whole group went on to discuss the problem. We then discussed the problem as a class and recorded data from each group's discussion. We continued to reinforce the vocabulary and strategies initiated in the Grange Hall Problem.

Our focus students gave us insights into the effectiveness of this initial stage of our unit. Natalie had completed the problem easily but showed very little explanation on her paper. This was not unusual. The class expectations for homework are loose. Students are expected to attempt the work, but it is not considered a finished product. We are more concerned with a student's experience and thoughts and trials than with carefully developed written explanations. Laramie had read and interpreted the problem incorrectly and didn't use square floors. However, we noticed that when he discussed his work with his group, he easily corrected his problem and found a generalization. It seemed obvious as we listened to the discussion at his table that he had just missed the word "square" in reading the problem. However, he was carefully creating tile floors and counting borders. Sari had a very systematic way of collecting the information on graph paper, and her neatly typed pattern description showed she certainly understood some of the concepts:

> Take any sized room and add up all the sides in feet. Then subtract four feet. You subtract four feet because you have to take into account the four corners. Since floor tiles are 1 ft. by 1 ft., this will give you the total squares around the perimeter of the room.
>
> —*Sari*

Yet Sari's work did not have a symbolic expression or sentence, an omission that did not necessarily reflect a lack of understanding on her part. We had wanted to make the task open-ended, and our directions had not specifically requested a symbolic rule. However, both Natalie and Sari reminded us that if we wanted evidence of process and understanding, we needed to explicitly ask students to provide it.

The student work, along with the group and full class discus-

sions, indicated that the students were beginning to build an understanding of the "process" perspective of functions. We were sat-
isfied that most students could consider a changing variable
situation like the pattern block chains or the graph paper floors
and gather and organize the data in a t-table. About half the students could begin to interpret their data, look for patterns, and verbally state the functional relationship between the ordered pairs.
However, only a few students could readily proceed to writing a
symbolic rule. Consequently we added an activity that used very
concrete materials and provided very regular data patterns for students to investigate.

Student work on this activity showed enough understanding for
us to move comfortably on to the next phase of instruction.

The next stage of our unit involved our most engaging activities:
"The Bottle Function,"[3] "Ball Bounce," and "Pendulums." These
lessons provided an opportunity to expand our students' understanding of functions. Because these activities stressed the graphical aspect of functions, we hoped that they would help to lay the
foundation for developing an "entity" perspective of functions,
seeing them not just as a recipe or rule but as a complete relationship. In each case, we began the activity with a focus question and
directions posed on the overhead projector. The Ball-Bounce lesson, our second activity in the series, began this way:

Question:

Is the rebound height a function of the drop height for a
ball that bounces?

Use the materials at your table to

a. conduct an experiment
b. collect data
c. make a graph on large paper
d. come to a conclusion

Be prepared to present your graph and conclusions to the
class.

Every member of the group should measure, record, and
participate in your group presentation.

For the ball-bounce problem, each table group was supplied with two meter sticks, a large piece of grid paper, and a tennis ball, a Ping-Pong ball, a Superball, or a standard rubber ball. It was becoming natural for us to initiate a lesson by having our students think about a question and then develop a plan to investigate it. We wanted to help them develop "habits of mind" that would allow them to become independent learners and logical thinkers. At this stage we were still guiding and modeling a plan for their work by giving specific directions for them to follow. We were also trying to increase their use of the vocabulary by wording the question "Is it a function of . . . ?" rather than "Is it dependent on . . . ?" In this activity, as in all three, the directions were designed to require every member of the group to collect, record, and graph the data. By giving them one large sheet of graph paper instead of individual sheets and by requiring all group members to take part in its presentation, we tried to foster interdependence and promote communication among the students.

We introduced the pendulum problem by simply holding a washer tied to a length of string and swinging it so that students could all see it. As we swung the washer, we asked the question, "What things might affect the swing time for a simple pendulum?" The students were quick to offer ideas: the amount of weight at the end of the string, the length of the string, the height you dropped it from. We decided it would be hard to measure the time for one swing using the second hand on the classroom clock. Consequently, the class decided to use ten swings as the constant to be timed. We asked each group to think about which ideas they wanted to investigate and to try to put their questions into words. With very little coaching, the students asked questions that excited us: "Is the swing time dependent on the length of the pendulum string? Is it dependent on the amount of weight used? Is it a function of the drop height?" As we planned this lesson, we were concerned that all the groups might want to do the same investigation, but we didn't have this problem. No more than two groups investigated any particular question.

Once again student products gave us important feedback. As the students worked through these early activities and the homework that accompanied them, we encountered one of our biggest dilemmas, one that we tackled throughout the unit and that was with us to the end. Our students were generally quite comfortable reading graphs, but lacked the skills and understanding for creating their own graphs. When we had the students predict the shape of the bottles that might have produced the sample graphs in the bottle activity, they drew sketches relatively easily. Furthermore, most students were able to do a straightforward homework assignment that asked them to analyze an assortment of graphs. However, when we gave them a homework assignment called "Pages in a Book," which we thought would follow the model we had created with the bottle function, we found that many students were still making common graphing errors. The problem asked students to conduct an experiment to determine whether the number of pages in a book was dependent on the book's thickness in centimeters. To conduct the experiment, students needed a ruler and at least ten books of different thicknesses. They were to record the total number of pages in each book, then measure the thickness of each book in centimeters. They them had to graph the results. The resulting student work helped us identify where students were still having difficulty representing functions. Despite our class discussions and modeling of graphing techniques and despite the coaching that we did with small groups and individuals during the unit, too many students continued to demonstrate misunderstandings. Some students, like Sari (Figure 2–2) and Zeben, incorrectly displayed their information as bar graphs, a representation with which they have the most experience. Students were used to counting and representing continuous quantities on bar graphs, e.g., to show answers to questions such as "How many students in the class are boys and how many are girls?" As they tried to answer the problem, they didn't see that in this situation the two numbers associated with each book (number of pages and thickness) represented a fixed relationships rather than a continuous quantity. Each pair represents only a single point on the graph, not the multiple points that a bar graph captures.

Other students, like Laramie (Figure 2–3), recorded information on their graphs based on the order in which it was collected. Thus,

FIGURE 2–2.

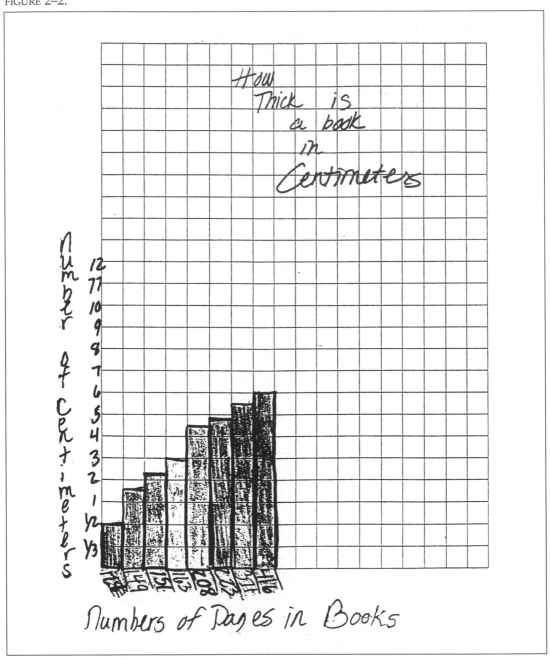

FIGURE 2–3.

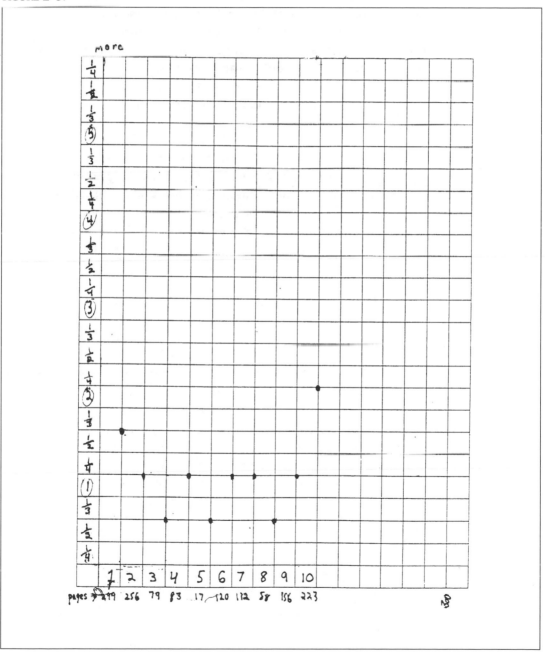

rather than establishing the x-axis as the "# of pages," they made it "the number of the book tested." This of course made it impossible to recognize any relationship between the numer of pages and the thickness of the book. We were completely baffled by this. We had not anticipated the extent of this confusion.

At this point we decided it was time for a "Fist to Five Self-Assessment." One of our constant concerns was trying to determine what and how much our students understood about functions and how well they were achieving the outcomes that we had posted on our wall chart. After completing and critiquing three class periods and a total of four activities and homework assignments, we gave the students a questionnaire for homework. The questionnaire used a five-finger scale as the standard with one indicating little understanding and five "really getting it." Most students rated themselves in the three- or four-finger range, and they voiced concerns about their lack of understanding about variables and drawing graphs.

As a second assessment, we also required every group member to complete an individual "Lab Report" and graph for their pendulum experiment even though they had already created a group graph on chart paper with a data table and conclusions (see Figure 2–3). These helped us document each student's progress toward understanding. We could see evidence that they were beginning to use the vocabulary to varying degrees. Sari wrote, "We found out that the shorter the string is, the less time it takes for 10 swings." Natalie recorded her prediction, "We thought the time was a function of the length," as well as her conclusion, "We found that the time of the swings is dependent on the length" (Figure 2–4). The students didn't overwhelm us with their confidence in their self-assessments, but we were pleased to see our modeling and language beginning to be reflected in their conversations and writings.

A marking period ended in the middle of our unit, so we had an opportunity for another assessment a short time later. After six classes and a total of eight different activities, Marcy asked her students to respond to some specific questions about functions in a letter to her as they organized and compiled their portfolios of

FIGURE 2–4.

MATH
Lab Report Form

Prediction/Hypothesis
What is it that you are testing? What is your prediction for the results of the experiment?

We are testing to see if the length is a function of the time, or the time is a function of the length.

We thought that the time was a function of the length but, since we went up in length by 5 inches at a time we thought that the time for each swing would increase by more than 2 or 3 seconds.

Procedure
What materials are you using? What rules are you following? Describe the <u>details</u> of your actions in doing this experiment. Draw a picture of your experiment design. Label it.

2 meter sticks, tape, markers, graph paper, pencils, and scribbled data.

We always used the same weight, the same height we dropped it from, we went up evenly by inches basically.

I would change the length of the pendulum while Donald kept the time, Jake graphed, I counted 10 swings. Jake and Donald wrote numbers while I graphed it.

pencil   Data   String

meter
sticks

FIGURE 2–4. *Continued*

Charting and/or Graphing of Results

Observations
What results did you find? What are the things that you notice about the results?
Anything peculiar or unexpected?

We found that the time of the swings is
dependent on the length. The time increased
by 1 or 2 and we thought it should be
more. So that was unexpected.

Conclusions
How do the results that you find compare to the expectations that you had before the
beginning of the experiment? Try to think of the reasons that the experiment
turned out the way it did.

Good. They matched up well.
You could kind of. tell before we even
started that the time was dependent on
the length.
       We checked all our info 2 and even
3 times so I'm pretty sure it's right.

their second-quarter work. The responses from our focus students indicate that students were still having a hard time with the abstract nature of functions.

NATALIE: I know that function means, dependent on. (or I think it does.) I know that functions tie into graphs, algebra, variables, and linear graphs although I'm not sure why. I know we must use functions out of school, at home, but I'm not sure how. I also don't know a plain, simple definition of the word function.

LARAMIE: Right now when you asked me about functions I seem to have forgotten about them kind of but what I know is that functions are what you can do in the process of math. I do not really know or I kind of get mixed up with what functions are and what they can do.

SARI: Functions I don't really understand that well, but I know that we have been dealing with graphs and that we experiment and we use probability a little bit. Like when we bounced the ball we made some guesses about it. One thing that I don't understand about this unit is what exactly is a function? I mean, I've learned now because I've paid attention but what is the complete definition of function?

Zeben didn't complete a letter.

These letters marked a significant juncture for us as teachers. As we read them, Marcy and I confronted again one of our most constant dilemmas: *Covering the concepts is easy, teaching for understanding is very, very hard!* Functions were unlike most other things students had learned about in their math classes. They weren't just operations to be performed, although they involved operations, and they weren't simply objects or things, like a radius or a parallelogram. It was clear from students' responses that trying to grasp both the entity and process aspects of functions simultaneously can make them somewhat elusive to students.

We knew that at any time we could give our students information and definitions, tell them what we wanted them to know, and have them take notes and then regurgitate their knowledge to us in a traditional quiz or a test. However, these letters demanded that we design additional activities that would help students continue to build on their previous experiences and expand their understanding of functions. From the activities we had done with pattern blocks and Cuisenaire® rods, we could see evidence of their ability to use symbols and to discover and represent pattern sentences. We could also observe them conducting experiments and using the language that we had modeled for them in the bottle function, the ball bounce, and the pendulum swing. They were experienced at collecting data and organizing it in a table, and when they worked together in small groups, they were likely to create appropriate scatter plots. They were beginning to get the idea of considering a line of best fit and thus identifying those relationships that might be linear functions. Still, they didn't seem to have the whole picture.

We decided to do at least one more lesson before giving the students their children's book challenge. We chose a function machine activity called "The U-Say, I-Say Game." The game is a version of "I'm thinking of a rule," where the leader creates a table of values by taking numbers contributed by students and performing the operation(s) of the mystery rule. As the activity continued, the students analyzed the table for patterns that they described in words and symbols.

We gave students the data in Figure 2–5 to graph individually.

As a whole class, we discussed students' findings and made a list of the relationships that students had discovered. We asked students to tell us in their own words the rule for the function machine. We charted all of the different ways in which students saw the rule on the overhead. Students' responses were diverse and showed us that even when it comes to computation not everyone sees things the same way:

> Take the U-say number and double it and then add one more to get the I-say number.
> U-say times two plus one is the I-say.
> Add the U-say to itself and then add one to get the I-say.
> Add one to U-say then add U-say to get the I-say.

We took this opportunity to emphasize once again the connection between tables, verbal and symbolic rules, and graphs on the coordinate plane. We also talked again about the difference between

FIGURE 2–5.

U-Say Independent	I-Say Dependent
3	7
8	17
-4	-7
5	11
9	19
7	15
2	5
-7	-13
4	9
1	3
-1	-1
0	1

"nice mathematics" and the fuzzier nature of "real world" mathematics that they may have experienced as they conducted their ball-bounce and pendulum experiments.

Finally we were ready for the culminating activity that we had laid out at the beginning of the unit. As the students were beginning their work on their children's books, Marcy and I encountered another dilemma: *There is never enough time to do everything you want to do.* We were rushed for time and consequently we didn't develop the process of creating the children's story in quite the way we had intended. We had originally planned to offer a selection list of explorations and experiments and have the groups either choose one from the list or create a related one of their own. Each team would then conduct its experiment or exploration, collect data, draw a graph and analyze its information for patterns, describe their results, and *then* create the children's story using this information. We thought this structure would keep mathematics at the center of the product. But we had already extended the unit several days beyond our schedule, and we would soon be interfering with a planned integrated winter survival unit. We decided to consolidate the instructions into one single challenge and present it to the students all at once.

As the children's books were nearing completion, we confronted yet another difficulty: *The performance doesn't always reveal what you intended.* We had thought that the children's book challenge would be a good way to assess our students' understanding of the concept of functions in a "nontraditional" way. We were excited when the language arts teacher agreed to integrate our activity into her curriculum and allow the students class time to work on the challenge there as well. We had even constructed a scoring rubric that we thought was flexible enough to evaluate both the language arts and the mathematics aspects of the products (Figure 2–6). We also asked students to complete self-assessment questionnaires that gave us feedback about their individual participation in the creation of their group's children's book. In addition, we solicited from students their judgment of their teammates' contributions.

Yet, as the books were being finished, we were simultaneously pleased with and disappointed by the students' work. In a class that submitted eight different stories, four stories showed a working knowledge of the concepts, three demonstrated a superficial understanding, and one missed the mark. We noticed that in the production of their storybook and their presentation to their classmates, the math content often took a backseat. The students were

FIGURE 2–6.

FUNCTIONS CHILDREN'S BOOK
GRADING RUBRIC

BOOK TITLE:_____

PUBLISHING COMPANY:_____   _____

TEXT

1. The story is complete and shows an attempt to deal with the concept of functions.
2. The story is interesting and complete. It features the concepts of functions and reflects *some* data gathered through research or exploration. The text is neat and has few errors.
3. The story *clearly* illustrates the concept of functions by featuring a *series of data* gathered through research or exploration. The text is interesting, clearly written, neat, and has few—if any—errors.

ILLUSTRATIONS/COVER

1. The book includes a cover and illustrations that go along with the text.
2. The book includes a well-designed, attractive cover. The illustrations are eye-catching and support the story.
3. The book includes a well-designed, attractive cover. The illustrations are neat, eye-catching, and support the text. Illustrations enhance the reader's understanding of functions.

very concerned about the language arts aspects of the project such as (1) writing a story that would interest small children; (2) keeping the concepts simple so that younger readers would understand them; and (3) creating illustrations that were colorful and eye-catching. As they focused on questions like "How do we do our drawings?," "How do we put it all together?," and "Do we need a title page?," they lost sight of the mathematics.

For example, during the planning time, Natalie's group had talked about developing the idea of pendulum swing time by telling a story about monkeys at the zoo that were alike in every way except for the length of their tails. They abandoned the idea when they decided that the drawings would be too difficult for them and settled on a very elementary idea: that the number of similar things that will fit into a closet is dependent on the size of the closet. The story that they created, "Sardines," was very well done. We could tell that they understood the concept, but they had really oversimplified it. In several other situations, we heard the students' conversations about their mathematical ideas as they were doing their initial planning, but their ideas did not appear in their final story.

Several groups chose to feature functions in an "Afterword" to their story. For example, Laramie's group wrote a story called "Jungle Panic" that featured the "Rumor Function," which we had done earlier in class. Their story was clever and colorful, and their last page revealed an increasing understanding of the concepts they had studied:

Afterword

You may think that this book is totally meaningless, and just a silly picture book. Actually, it deals with a very sophisticated subject. Functions. A function is basically a rule. Take this book, for example. It starts off that only one animal knows about the fictitious hunter. He tells two more animals, then leaves to go about his business. The two animals each go off and proceed to tell two more animals, then leave. It goes on this way (each animal telling two more, then leaving) for a while, until the end of the book. What is actually happening is that the number of animals is doubling each time a new set of animals know. We have attached a data sheet of this information. Hopefully, after reading this book, you will be more familiar with functions and how they affect your daily life.

Minutes	Animals
10	2
20	4
30	8
40	16
50	32
60	64

As this example shows, the unit netted us some results and some more questions. When the students write, "A function is basically a rule," we see evidence of the development of their understanding of functions from a process perspective. They continue by describing the rule as "doubling each time," and they have included their data table to support that rule. They still do not seem ready to move to a symbolic representation of their rule, and they may be viewing the rule from a vertical change aspect in their table. We were interested to note that although we had done a similar activity in class that had included drawing and describing a graph of the data, these students chose not to include that here or in their children's story. We're not sure why.

As we looked at the children's stories, we realized they didn't tell us enough about the students' understanding of functions. In addition, they were group projects, and we wanted some individual accountability. Consequently, Marcy and I decided to add an additional culminating activity. We designed the "Ramp Height P.O.W." (Problem of the Week) to address these concerns. In this problem, we asked students to conduct an exploration that would determine if the distance that an object rolls down a ramp is dependent on the height of the ramp. The problem did give us evidence of the students' skills (and misunderstandings) in conducting an experiment, collecting, recording, and graphing data, and, to some extent, their understanding of a linear relationship. It also prompted students to make predictions and analyze their data and graphs. In Sari's work (Figure 2–7), we see examples of this,

FIGURE 2–7. *Sari's Ramp Height Conclusions*

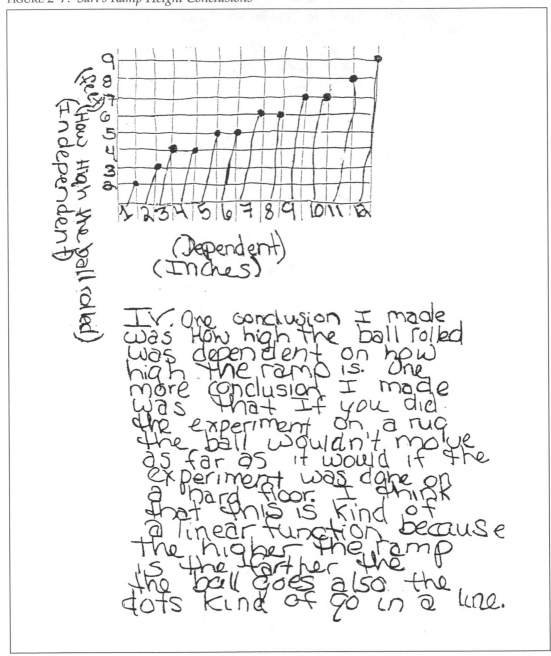

including an interesting graph. There is evidence in her words and graphing of lingering confusion mixed with emerging understanding. Although many of our students incorrectly graphed the height of the ramp along the vertical axis and the rolling distance along the horizontal axis, she has chosen her axes appropriately, but then she calls the rolling distance independent. We were also surprised to see the reflected layout of her axes. We surmised that because she seemed to have collected her data from high to low ramp height, this may have influenced her graphing strategy.

Marcy and I have talked several times about what we would do differently with this unit next time. In retrospect, we would definitely make the children's book challenge less open-ended by having the groups choose from a list of suggested explorations as we had originally planned. We would also have the students complete their mathematical investigations *before* beginning work on their children's book and suggest that they aim their story at fourth- and fifth-grade students to avoid the dilemma of choosing story lines that were too simple to demonstrate their real knowledge and understanding. We would build in intermediate deadlines for completion of stages of the work, in order to give the groups more frequent and appropriate feedback. We attempted to circulate while questioning, coaching, and advising throughout the time the students were working on the project, but it wasn't possible to keep track of how they were implementing any changes that might have been discussed. Some might ask, why keep the book challenge if writing it takes so much time? Isn't that time away from math? Yet when the students were asked what they liked best about the unit, it was unanimous. They really enjoyed doing the children's book challenge. Natalie: "It was fun coming up with your own functions and it's real open and you get to be creative with it." Zeben: "The children's book has been a lot of fun. We're doing a story about how big a crayon box is is dependent on the number of crayons you want to put in it." One of our original goals was to make functions meaningful to our students. The book challenge had done that.

Marcy is also talking about revisiting functions later in the spring when she introduces the use of graphing calculators. Based on our review of students' work, we believe that many of the students are right on the verge of pulling it all together. When Natalie was asked, in a taped interview with the science facilitator, "What has been the hardest thing you encountered in the functions unit?," she replied: "Trying to grasp the whole idea. I still can't give you a definition, but I think I can give examples. At first, the terminology was hard and nobody got it. And trying to stay focused was hard, but it started to sink in after a while and we could see that variables, and "dependent on," and "being a function of" something, and linear graphs are all connected." And Laramie said: "A function is something that is dependent on something else and most of the time it's measurable. You collect information and you graph it to show independent and dependent variables like in the Rumor Problem."

We also tried to assess how well our unit helped students develop the ability to view the world mathematically. This is a hard call. When asking students questions like, "Why are functions important? Why should people know about functions?," we got a wide variety of responses. Natalie said, "Well, I don't know. Sometimes you learn things in school that you never use, unless you have a job in that area. I don't know how we're going to use this, but I know it will come up in algebra and other math classes." Later in the interview, she said, "Our group really got into the ball bounce experiment. We first tried it on the carpet and it didn't come out real well, I mean, we got a line of best fit OK, but we tried it again on the table where the surface was hard and we got better results."

Zeben also commented on the ball bounce: "So we did a ball-bounce thing in class and if you're a stunt man, what you learned about ball-bouncing surfaces would be important. If you're landing on a pad and you don't get it right you could get hurt." Zeben's group had experimented on several surfaces and were impressed when the ball scarcely bounced at all when they used two books as their landing surface. He also said, "If you were driving a train, how fast you could stop depends on your speed." But when he was asked about the occurrence of functions in real life and around home, he quickly replied, "No, I don't use functions in my home."

Despite the difficulties and uncertainties of helping real kids learn real mathematics, we will continue to use and revise this unit. We think of it as a "work in progress." We're already thinking ahead to next year. In addition to the possible changes that we've already mentioned, we want to ensure more reflection time. One of the things that Marcy and I struggle to do in our teaching is provide our students with meaningful opportunities to reflect on what they are learning and to construct their knowledge from what they experience. We tend to fill nearly every moment of our classes with things for kids to do, and when we're pressed for time the thing we sacrifice is time to think and make journal entries. These old habits are hard to break.

The process of revisiting and revising a previous unit has kept us growing as teachers. Our focus on four students kept us honest. Overall, we were pleased. Our skills in designing an outcome-driven curriculum are improving. When I asked Marcy what the major differences were between last year's teaching of functions and this year's, she replied: "Our focus has changed. Last year we were more concerned with covering the skills and concepts. This year we are much more concerned with what the outcomes are and what understanding may look like. It isn't that we *weren't* looking at outcomes and understanding last year, but there has been a shift in emphasis in our strategies. Despite the fact that we used very similar activities, we seemed to be *presenting* the topic last year, while this year we were much more likely to be facilitators of learning and to be much more tuned in to the progress and difficulties that students were having." We agreed that we are making progress in assessing student understanding, but that we have a long way to go. We believe our students are gaining an intuitive knowledge of functions and are beginning to have moments when they view the world "with mathematical eyes." That is our greatest reward, and that is what will keep us refining and revising what we do in the classroom.

Notes

1. New Standards. 1995 Circulation Draft. *Performance Standards: Vol. 2. Middle School.* (Available from New Standards, 700 Eleventh St. NW Suite 750, Washington, DC 20001)
2. E. Phillips. 1991. *Patterns and Functions.* Reston, VA: National Council of Teachers of Mathematics.

Finding a Place for Functions in the Science Classroom

Exploring the Respiratory System

Carrie Wong

First There Are Questions

"Why are you here?" was the first question put to us when we first met for the *Curriculum Seminars* at Harvard in December of 1994. Why was I here? I had abandoned my students, who tearfully begged me not to leave them yet *again* for another conference, this time in the middle of the week when we were deep in the trenches of science fair planning. Before leaving San Francisco, I had frantically planned for the substitute, taken a red-eye flight across three time zones, and then sprained my ankle the first night in Cambridge. My only thought was *why am I here?!?*

As I sat there feeling guilty, miserable, and quite sorry for myself, I contemplated this question. I started to think about Antoine. On the day I left, he had just looked at me and said softly, "Don't go." I almost burst into tears. Of all my students, I figured Antoine would be the last to notice I was even gone. I didn't believe he would care one way or the other. How often I overlook or forget the "quiet ones" who hear me, but to whom I don't always take the time to listen. Unfortunately, in my overcrowded classroom, I sometimes find myself expecting things only from students who expect something from me. But now Antoine had made contact; he had crossed the line. He overcame his fears, his insecurities, his attitudes to let me know that he wanted his teacher to be there for him. Following his example, I now needed to overcome my issues and approach the curriculum seminars with openness and motivation to learn. If I wanted my students to be lifetime learners, then I had to pave the way. I needed to put aside my feelings of regret at making the commitment to take part in the curriculum seminars, and look at what I might get out of this experience.

Slowly I became aware that this whole thing might not be half bad. It was refreshing being the student rather than the teacher, especially when I could engage in hands-on experiences but was not responsible for the setup. I took a deep breath, tried to forget my throbbing ankle, and turned my attention to the overhead projector on which Ron Ritchhart had just let fall the first drop of a curious green liquid. Hey, this professional development stuff might just turn out to be fun.

The puddle of green liquid grew and so did my curiosity. Ron had instructed us to watch carefully and take notes on what we saw as he performed a simple experiment. I became intrigued as I watched Ron slowly release drop after green drop onto the overhead projector. In the projector's light the translucent liquid rippled and a dark ring formed around a puddle, which grew larger with each drop. I recorded my observations in my notebook and waited to find out what would come of this demonstration.

When we moved into a discussion of what each of us had seen, I was amazed by the detail and diversity of the group's observations: the ripples, the color of the liquid, the number of drops released, the size of the puddle, the refraction of the light within the puddle. I was also impressed by the connections we were making. There were both simple relationships to be explored, such as the size of the puddle as a result of the number of drops of liquid, and complex ones, like the intensity of the color as a function of the curve of the puddle. Gradually, Ron guided our water puddle discussion into a more teacher-conscious conversation about learning. I realized how this activity could be used to show the differences between observation and opinion or between description and analysis. A teacher could use it to introduce the mathematical concepts of functions and dependent and independent variables by building on the natural vocabulary students used to describe the event. The activity also offered practice for collecting, interpreting, and analyzing data. There was a wealth of opportunities to teach math and science skills in the simple act of dripping out little drops of colored water!

After being wowed, the group and I began to face some drab realities. Is an understanding of functions really attainable for our students? How do you teach higher-order thinking skills to students who don't even have a full range of computation skills? How can I expect students to collect and graph numerical data if they can't even add or subtract properly? A majority of the students in my classroom had little understanding of grouping or sorting numbers and limited knowledge of place values. They could barely name the four basic mathematical operations. How in the world was I going to teach them to collect data, identify and measure variables, and graph on horizontal and vertical axes? A debate raged within me as my thinking went back and forth between what Ron had just modeled for us and my own view of the challenges that awaited me back in my classroom. I was engaged and amazed by all that Ron showed us could happen during our learning experiences, but functions still seemed so far out of reach. Would I really be able to teach such a powerful concept effectively to my kids? Could I really accomplish this kind of work in my classroom?

Looking for Meaningful Connections

The conversations begun in Cambridge and the lessons learned there stayed with me as I returned to my classroom in San Francisco. I had learned to see functions as mathematically empowering tools useful in decision making. Gradually, I began to notice mathematical relationships all around me. A dripping faucet may not at first appear to be a big deal, but once you see it as a function of water loss over time, you realize that gallons of wasted water are going down the drain. And if you've ever experienced a six-year California drought, you can see the value of understanding this function and the importance of fixing the faucet to conserve this precious resource. I wanted my students to understand, interpret, and interact with our mathematical world as well. I wanted them to have a real basis for good decision making. Being able to identify functional relationships between variables and understand their impact on a particular situation would push my students to the realization that real choices yield real results.

I realized that I should not limit my students' learning just because they lacked skills in certain areas. I knew my students could understand the impact of that dripping faucet. Such simple experiences could provide the access I needed to develop the concept of functions. I wanted to give my students the best foundation possible for future study, and that meant more than memorizing facts from the science textbook and applying computational algorithms. A wide range of concepts and skills could be addressed powerfully through the use of functions: observation, experimentation, research, communication, interpretation, analysis, synthesis, problem solving, and critical thinking. Furthermore, if I made the work accessible, engaging, and meaningful, I should be able to support my students in developing rich mathematical and scientific understanding.

I was already a month behind in both math and science when I began considering whether and how to teach functions. I had spent a great deal of time in the beginning of this school year building confidence in math by giving my students a basic foundation for understanding numbers. I was supposed to be teaching fractions, decimals, percentages, and ratios and should have at least started on one system of the human body. But making my students feel comfortable with talking about math came first. With all of these pressures in mind, I struggled with how I was going to teach my students about functions along with everything else my district mandated. You know the expression "less is often more"? Maybe now was the time to try that perspective. Maybe I should consider incorporating functions into my class as a way to explore more deeply the concepts I had already taught, rather than as an unrelated addition. If I developed good learning and study skills and gave my students powerful tools, then students could take the skills they acquired and use them to continue learning. Instead of teaching students superficial information, I would take one idea and show students how to study it in much more depth.

I had been trying to integrate my math and science curricula, but even strong, natural connections were hard to see because the content for both subjects was so strictly outlined by my district. I had been incorporating simple math activities, like measuring, into my science program, but now I had something a little more advanced. How could functions be used to better understand the human body? Health issues and choices were a major part of our study of the human body. And how *do* people make health decisions? By identifying the causes or indicators. Voilà! Students could use functions to identify variables that may affect their health or parts of their bodies. Making students aware of how their choices can affect their health and teaching them the tools to prove it mathematically sounded great to me. It was real. It was powerful.

Now that I had a perspective, I still had to narrow down my scope to fit into a unit. I decided to focus on one system of the body. I had recently read an article in a national magazine that included statistics showing a recent rise in the number of teenage smokers. This helped me make my final connection between functions and a science topic. Our overview of the respiratory system would include investigations into the variables that affect lung capacity, the amount of air held by the lungs at one time, with an emphasis on smoking.

Using Functions to Make Science Learning More Powerful

After a preassessment activity and some introductory pictures of healthy and diseased lungs, I introduced two activities about breathing: *breathing rate* and *measuring lung capacity*. I had taught these activities in the past, and I knew that they would help develop the major concepts that students needed to know in order to understand the difference between how fast and how much we breathe. However, before I was exposed to the power of functions, this was where the unit always stopped. The activities helped students acquire a basic understanding of the concepts, but they did not allow student learning to go anywhere. Students didn't make scientific discoveries or formulate hypotheses; they merely learned facts. The reality was that these activities had always been unsatisfying for me and for the students. To my delight, when I incorporated functions, our study of the respiratory system took on new depth as we designed and conducted experiments to explore the factors that affect lung capacity.

My class used these two activities to begin their investigation of whether or not there was a functional relationship between breathing rate and lung capacity. In our initial discussion, most students felt that a person with a fast breathing rate must have a small lung capacity—that is what would force them to breath a lot. However, a few students were not sure the two were related at all. I asked students how we would go about answering these questions. We discussed the need to collect some data to see if we would be able to draw any conclusions. I sent students home that night with a recording sheet and asked them to collect data on the breathing rate of their family members and then graph the result. Through this first assignment, I wanted students to get some practice collecting and analyzing simple data before we jumped into exploring functions. We had been working on basic graphing skills, and my students were gradually becoming more adept at reading graphs and asking questions about them. They were coming to see graphs as communication vehicles. I wanted to see what questions they would generate based on these early graphs.

The next day, as we prepared for our class discussion, I noticed that only a few students had created graphs and several had forgotten their homework. Nonetheless, students shared their information (see Figure 3–1), and I began to push them to interpret the data and formulate some initial hypotheses. For the most part, the class data were tightly clustered in the teens, but there was something of a range. To encourage kids to think about connecting variables and to consider cause-and-effect relationships, I asked them to think about what might account for the range in the number of breaths per minute. Why might breathing rate differ across individuals? The most common response at this point was age.

Next, we moved to a discussion of lung capacity, again considering it initially as a single isolated variable. Using balloons, we devised a simple proxy for measuring lung capacity. I explained that since lung capacity was the amount of air our lungs would hold,

FIGURE 3–1. *Corey Lau's "Breaths in a Minute" Graph*

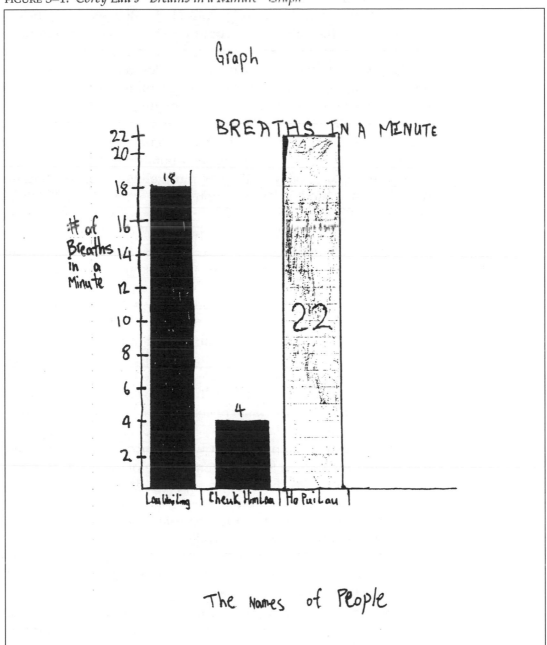

breathing a single breath into a balloon would be a good way to measure how much air our lungs could hold. By measuring the circumference of the balloon, we could obtain an easy measurement that we could use to make comparisons. Students had a good time working with partners to collect data. After generating some descriptive statistics, such as the average lung capacity and the range, I asked students if they thought lung capacity was connected to breathing rate. Some students were convinced that breathing rate and lung capacity were connected. They reasoned that since the smaller members of their families had smaller lungs, they would take more breaths per minute. Many other students were confused by the whole notion of any connection. This was our first real attempt to talk about cause-and-effect relationships, and some students had difficulty making the connections I was pushing them toward. However, I was pleased that some students had not only identified a functional relationship but had also been able to express it verbally in narrative form.

To begin to make the connection between breathing rate and lung capacity, I had students collect data on both breathing rate and lung capacity from four members of the class. I then asked them to describe the relationship between the data they had collected (see Figure 3–2). This turned out to be much harder for students than I had anticipated. Although I had pointed out the similarities between our data collection and our work with function machines in math class, many students couldn't make the connection. Math was math and this was science. In addition, there was not much variation in the circumference of the balloons across individuals, so it was difficult for students to identify a relationship and draw any conclusions. Some students looked at their small data table and said that the circumference of the balloon was double the breaths per minute. While this was true for some data, it didn't consider the data in its entirety. Furthermore, for those students who had anticipated a connection, the data did not readily confirm their initial hypothesis.

Student difficulties like these actually provided the basis for an important discussion about data collection, organization, and interpretation. Examining the data they collected at home and com-

FIGURE 3–2. *Steven Zhao's "Breathing: Getting Air into the Body"*

Name: **Steven Zhao**   Date: **5 - 15 - 95**

Science Notebook Page

Breathing: Getting Air into the Body — page 3

4. *Lung Capacity*

How Much Do You Breathe?

How much air do you think you hold in one breath? To find out, inhale as much air as you can, and then exhale into a balloon. Tie the balloon. Using string and then the ruler, measure the circumference of the balloon.

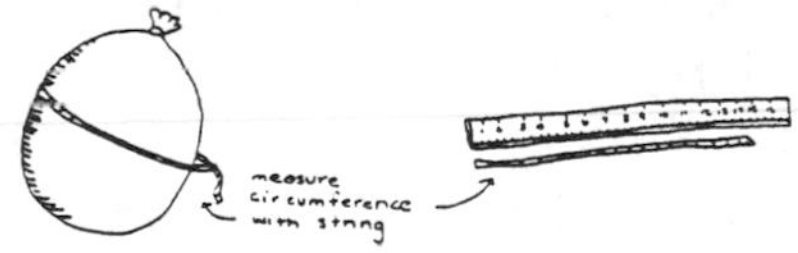

measure
circumference
with string

Record the circumference of your balloon here **55**

5. *Group Data*

Fill in the following data for your group.

Group Member	Average Breaths/Minute	Circumference of Balloon with Exhaled Air
1 *Mauricio*	29	50
2 *Steven*	32	55
3 *Joseph*	18	57
4 *Aurdrey*	24	57
Group Average		

What relationship, if any, can you see between breathing rate and how much air can be held in one breath?

It's double.

paring it to what we collected in class, students realized that we had less variation in our classroom in terms of both lung capacity (as represented by the circumference of a balloon) and breaths per minute. They hypothesized that this might be influencing our interpretation. I took this opportunity to introduce students to scatter plots. We had done some basic work on coordinate graphing, and students were familiar with how to plot points. However, we had not used this method much. Collecting data from all of the members of the class, I created one large class graph. With the combined data displayed in a graph rather than a table, students could now see a slight negative relationship between breathing rate and lung capacity. Eventually, our discussion of the initial data on breathing rates and lung capacity led students to identify other physical and biological variables that might influence lung capacity, such as age, height, weight, and gender.

Using the scientific method of experimentation, we did some activities in which students formed hypotheses and then collected data in order to make conclusions about possible physical influences on lung capacity. Students worked in groups to collect data both at home and at school and then to organize it into a graph. Each person had to collect data on ten people. Groups were allowed to choose the same variable to research. Students had no problem making scatter plots and creating graphs with appropriate labels, but they still had difficulty expressing their findings in words. Amaoge's graph (Figure 3–3) shows a scatter plot of age and lung capacity. The dots are correctly placed and labeled, but no conclusions are stated. However, in conversation he was able to identify a positive relationship between age and lung capacity. He said that the graph appeared to be really two different graphs, one of kids and one of adults. The relationship between lung capacity and age was easier to see for kids than for adults.

Students displayed their group graphs around the room, and each group presented its findings. In the class presentations, students were able to identify basic relationships and express informally the functional relationships they saw. During the discussions that followed each presentation, a whole slew of questions, inferences, analyses, and rich comments came out. For example, when

FIGURE 3–3. Amaoge's "Comparing Lung Capcity"

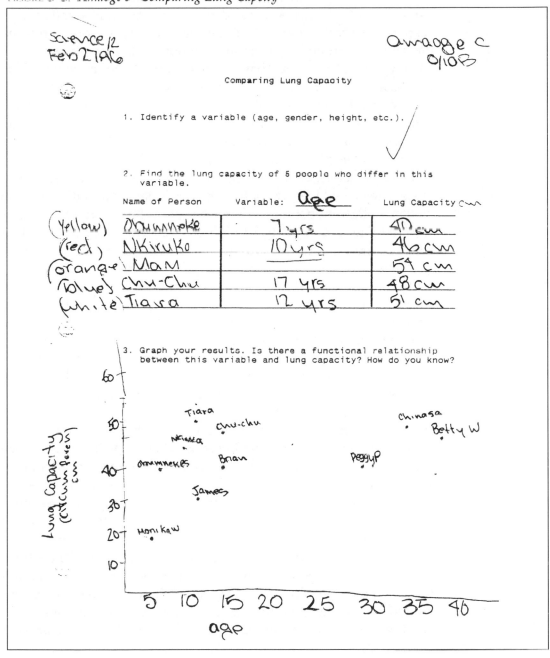

we looked at two different graphs that displayed the data on the same variable, someone noticed that the functional relationships were easy to see on one but not on the other. This brought out the concept of "outliers" that disrupt the flow of the graph and muddle the view of the "line that best fits." These "troublemakers," as my class referred to them, were caused by other variables that may have distorted the effect of the particular variable being studied. They now knew the reasoning behind a *controlled* experiment: the importance of isolating a variable to truly test its influence.

Once students had a basic understanding of the influence of physical factors on lung capacity, I introduced the parts of the respiratory system, reviewed the path of the air, and explained about the gas exchange—all in preparation for our study of the environmental factors affecting lung capacity. In addition, we went over a fact sheet on tobacco, and I did a demonstration to simulate what happens inside the lungs when a person smokes. This was the same information I had given kids when I taught the unit in the past—the same basic information that is imparted to kids at this age to scare them away from smoking. However, we all know from statistics on teenage smokers that the information itself often has little effect. I wanted to use the idea of functions to make the message more memorable. So, after we went through the information, we set out as a class to collect data on the lung capacity of smokers and nonsmokers.

The most meaningful experience came during the data collection process. A pair of students had used a white balloon to collect data from a smoker. They had been amazed and disgusted to see the person's yellowish breath shallowly fill the balloon. I had previously demonstrated the "Smoking Lung in a Bottle." Besides being disgusted by the lung's smell and physical appearance, students were shocked by its diminished capacity. If seeing the lung and the yellow balloon doesn't convince students that smoking has long-term effects, nothing will. After graphing their findings in class, we stood back and examined the results. Even though there was a range of lung capacity for both groups, which we concluded was due to the other variables at work, smokers had a considerably lower range of lung capacity than their nonsmoking counterparts. Students were then encouraged to reflect on the data and draw some conclusions about the effects of smoking, which they put into a letter to a smoker.

Reflecting on Learning

Children copy what they see. They follow after their friends, their older siblings, other adults in the community, and their parents. This is a lot to counteract. You just can't preach to teenagers and expect them to take your warning to heart. However, the emphasis on functional relationships and the respiratory system allowed students to examine the relationship between an assortment of variables and lung capacity. Consequently, students proved to themselves the hazards and consequences of certain choices. The many hands-on experiences and demonstrations were powerful and made an impact on students. You can see this below as Steven, a nonnative English speaker, expresses his enthusiasm in his end-of-unit journal reflection.

Journal on Respiratory System
When we started the respiratory system, it was difficult to understand the function and learn the parts. But of the many work require and many fascinating activities we did in class, learning about the respiratory system got much better and fun. I really enjoy this assignment. Learning and not learning about this system is a big difference because it gives me a step ahead of learning this system later year, and it may also help me understand other system more better. And best of all, I got this valuable knowledge in my brain which I felt really happy. You know, I really like how you explain about the respiratory system to me. For example, you give many activities and demonstrations about the lung and many assignment to encourage me to learn. Before, I used to read a book about human body. But after a few days, I forget about it. But you teaching it to me is a BIG DIFFERENCE!

Steven Zhao

What amazed me the most from this unit was the quality of the conversations I had with my students. We had some stimulating discussions on how multiple variables may influence lung capacity and what kind of experimental design it would take to isolate a single one. They also learned more about how math can be used as a tool to make better decisions. The mathematical power of functions made informed decision making possible for my students. It helped develop their sense of personal and social responsibility. I had to admit: it looked as if my time out of the classroom back in December had been worth it, for both me and my students.

4

Math Curse Revisited

Seeing Math in Many Places

Amy Benedicty and Sean Donahoe

How the Math Curse Came to Haunt Amy

As an adult I returned to college to study math. I remember it vividly. My husband told me, "You're going to love calculus—it will make you look at the world in a whole new way." So I dutifully did my textbook problems. I even enjoyed a fair amount of success. But several months into calculus I had to admit I didn't feel any dramatic new perspective on the world coming over me. Boldly, I asked my husband for an example. He replied, "Well, every time you turn on the faucet!" So I went to the kitchen, turned on the faucet, and waited. Concentrate as I might, it was the same old faucet. I simply could not see the calculus pouring out the spigot!

So when, in our functions seminar, I was told that middle school students could come to see the world through "math eyes," I wondered if it were really so. Still, the idea that we could do concrete activities with our middle school students that would enhance their chances for later success in more abstract high school algebra classes appealed to me. I liked the idea of demystifying the specialized vocabulary of "independent and dependent variables." I left the seminars convinced that in order for my students to reach the goals of becoming powerful users of math and controlling math as a means to having more choices in the world—they, and I, would need to explore challenging concepts like functions. But all the questions teachers learn to ask kept churning in my mind. For instance, was it wise to teach a unit that was at least a year ahead of the usual district curriculum to students whose basic math skills lagged many years behind the seventh-grade curriculum? And there was that faucet: how could I, as a teacher who lacked well-developed "math vision" herself, guide students to develop such vision?

Functions: A First Round

One day in late May toy stations greeted students when they came to my math class. At one station students could send toy cars down ramps from different angles; at another they could observe bouncing balls; at a third they could play with view tubes. Each station was an opportunity to stage experiments and collect data. For example, the car ramp station consisted of a toy car, a white vinyl building gutter hinged to form a ramp and a track, and a wooden ladder with rungs at five-centimeter intervals. By placing the ramp on the rungs at different heights, the students could predict and observe how the steepness of the ramp affected the distance the car would travel down the track. Even the most skeptical students did not consider themselves too sophisticated to enjoy the activities. As they did, important mathematical principles and important information about my students' math performance began to emerge. Take Tanya's work. When you look at her data collection and graphing of a toy car running down a ramp and along a track, you realize that she sees the particulars of the physical world she is trying to represent mathematically, that she is working with numbers, words, and graphic representations for the same physical events (see Figure 4–1). You also see that she has an incipient understanding of such fundamentals as prediction and variable rates of change: she forecasts what will happen at each higher rung on the ramp—unless you set it vertically, in which case the car will simply fall to the ground. However, even as Tanya does all this "mathematical seeing," she still grapples with the rules and conventions

FIGURE 4–1. *Tanya's Work*

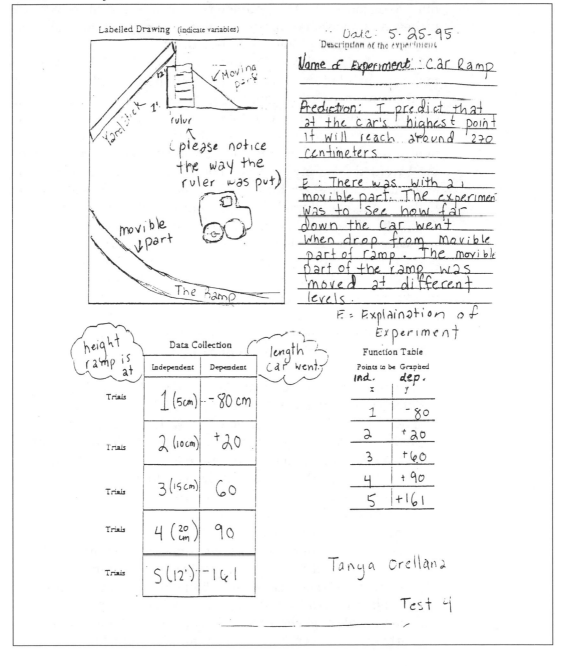

of mathematics like many of my students. She has her first car running a distance of –80 centimeters, she mixes centimeters and inches, and she marks her y-axis not into regular intervals on a scale but with data points she collected.

But engaged and busy as my students were, something was missing. I handed students a data collection form including spaces for drawing, predicting, tabulating, graphing, and writing a conclusion. It was the same one I had been using for years.[1] But this time, when I looked at those sheets through my gradually opening math eyes, I realized how much more than collecting and recording I wanted from my students. For example, there was no space anywhere on the sheet for prediction—even though that was key to their understanding. Even after I modified the form by putting a "Prediction" heading in the "description of experiment" space, it was easy for students to miss. I used Ron Ritchhart's ink blob and bottle activities from our seminar to push predicting.[2] My students were amenable. When I reminded them to make predictions and to measure several times to ensure accuracy, they did. But the greater problem was that I had not thought through the most basic question: "What elements contribute to a meaningful prediction?" An entry from my teaching journal makes this clear:

> We had a class discussion about useful prediction. One of the defects of the lab record sheet was that it had no specific space for prediction; rather, students were to include the prediction under "description of experiment." Next time I do this unit I will make a separate space for "prediction" and include some leading questions: Do you think the increase will be at regular intervals? at proportionally larger or smaller intervals? This part definitely needs some clarifying in my mind and some scaffolding for students. Specific criteria could be developed for what makes good prediction.
>
> I had observed that many students made very specific predictions as to how far a car or ball would go but did not generalize a prediction. We discussed some examples from their journals of generalized predictions—but there was a dearth of good ones. No one, for example, predicted

increases or decreases by proportional amounts. I'm still not certain how to teach this.

Perhaps the problem lies in the *purpose*—why do we care about the result? For what reason are we predicting?

Looking back now, I see how much more use I could have made of the toy activities to help students understand the relationship between their play with concrete objects, their graphic pictures of those events, and the formal numerical representations of both the events and the relationships. For instance, Tanya's work with the ramp and car generates the function $f(x) = 11 \cdot (x - 5)$. Deriving that would have required students to learn about the y-intercept, and I felt too pressed by time—it was the last week in May when I started the toy stations—and too overwhelmed to teach it. Now I would design my function toys differently, choosing ones that could all yield those kinds of abstract, but direct, representations of events. For instance, I might well skip the game of finding at which point a ruler will slide off the table when counterbalanced by increasing numbers of pennies. Fun as it is, it results in $f(x) = [29 \cdot (7/24)x + (30 \div 2)] \div [1 + (7/24)x]$.

Even with all this evidence about how physical events can engage and challenge students to create meaningful visual and numeric representations, the teacher in me wanted students to move from "just playing with function toys" to working with the more abstract "function machine game" where students input an x value into a chalkboard "function machine," are told the resulting y value, and then have to guess what function has acted upon the x value to give the y value as a result. For example, inputting 3 and coming out with a 4 could give a function of $f(x) = x + 1$.

But the connection between these "pure" exercises and the earlier toy activities was not clear at all to my students. I discovered this when some of my strongest students came to lunch-time study hall to clarify the homework. For homework the students had to invent five functions according to certain parameters, e.g., use a fraction such as $f(x) = x \cdot \frac{1}{2}$ or use an exponent such as x^3. Then they had to choose five x values to input into each of their functions and graph them to see what the curve would look like. Marlon Escobar chose to graph x^2, though he chose only one negative x value so he did not see the full parabola (Figure 4–2).

At the time I noted:

> Several of my quickest students came to lunch tutoring because they wanted further clarification of the assignment. They were especially unclear about how the input and output values of the function machine translated to the values in the t-table and how these in turn translated to the graph coordinates. These same students had had no difficulty translating the data values of the toy activities to tables and graphs. It was interesting that they had trouble making this connection, although after the tutoring session they had no trouble. Probably I didn't model it enough. The "grapevine" clarified the assignment for about 60 percent of the students but the homework results showed that many students did not even attempt the assignment. Usually about 90 percent of the students at least attempt an assignment. End-of-the-year-itis was probably a factor, also.

Looking back now, I would credit another factor as well. The invent-a-function work was also the most formal and most distant from the aim of seeing the world through math eyes. It was an attempt to bridge to algebra conventions that was probably premature.

I decided to make the final project a children's book. On the one hand, I was simply remembering the success of similar projects my language arts classes had done in the past with storybook themes, and the pleasure of taking a walking field trip through the Mission on a warm June day to present the books at a local elementary school. I remembered how the younger children brought out the most tender instincts in the very middle school students who try to project the toughest demeanors. I didn't have a clear idea of the format for the function books but devised some criteria:

1. **The booklet would be aimed at an audience of fourth or fifth graders.** The purpose of aiming the book at this level was to allow my students to practice using the technical vocabulary they

FIGURE **4–2.** *Marlon Escobar's Homework*

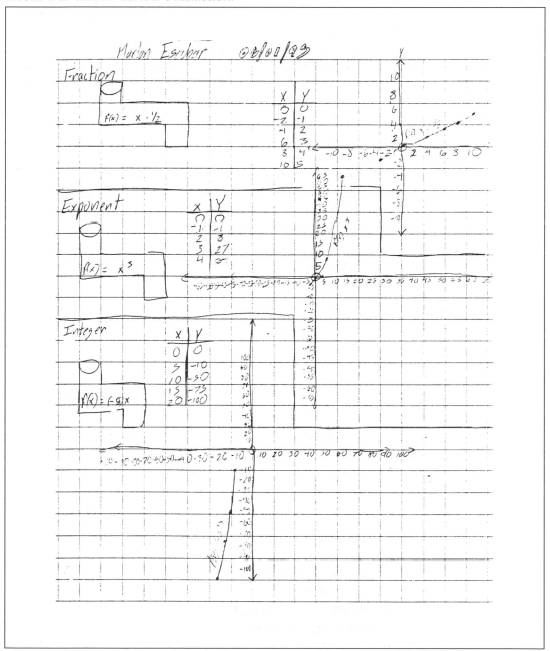

had learned while studying functions; I couldn't see students below fourth grade being able to handle this vocabulary as readers.

2. **Certain vocabulary words had to be included:** *function, variable, independent and dependent variable, x-coordinate, y-coordinate, etc.* We generated class definitions for each word. Some students wanted to use definitions from a math book glossary or the dictionary, but we read a few and decided these would not be intelligible to fourth or fifth graders; they were barely, if at all, intelligible to us! I had latched on to Ron Ritchhart's comment that gaining familiarity with these words now would make formal algebra books less intimidating in high school, and I wanted the students to reinforce their facility with these words by using them in their books.

3. **The booklet had to include a graph and a table, as well as verbal explanations to ensure that students would make connections among all these forms of representing data.**

When students came into class next time, they found on their tables a selection of children's math books on various topics from both the library and my personal collection. These included books by Leonard Everett Fisher, such as *Number Art* and *Calendar Art*; books from the Young Math Books series published by Thomas Crowell, New York, including James Fey's *Long and Short, High Low, Thin, Wide*; and Robert Froman's *Rubber Bands, Baseballs, and Doughnuts: A Book About Topology*. I also included all of Mitsumasa Anno's books, including *Anno's Mysterious Multiplying Jar*.[3] A writing prompt asked students to list at least five elements that made the books appealing to children. Their lists included the following:

- large type
- colorful pictures
- pictures that look like cartoons
- questions to get the kids involved
- games and problems
- not too much writing on each page
- examples that appeal to kids
- activities for kids to try

We made a composite list and these became further criteria for
the books. The homework was to think about how such a book
might look. Actually, I had no clear vision of the books students
might create. I expected most of them would describe a toy experiment from the ones the students had done in class. But the
students came up with better ideas.

When I asked them for their ideas the next day, Cameron Carter
raised his hand and said, "My book is going to be about birthday
parties. The function is $n+1$ because you always get a present from
everyone you invite plus your mother gives you one, too." Thanks
to Cameron's initial idea, the other students buzzed with possibilities. Several of the final products demonstrated an understanding
of functions; two, *Pinocchio's Nose* (Figures 4–3 and 4–4) and *Graph
Your Cupcakes*, succeeded as fairly polished children's books. All
could have served as diagnostic tools to guide future teaching if it
weren't the last week of school.

Yet for all the richness of the final products, they still left me
with some unresolved questions, both about the project and about
the unit as a whole. When I planned the unit, I had aimed for three
things. First, I felt the students needed many nonthreatening,
hands-on activities to begin to see functions and to feel comfortable with vocabulary such as "independent variable" and "dependent variable" that might intimidate many of them if they first
encountered it in the abstraction of an algebra text. I wanted students to gain from these activities the ability to describe functional
relationships in a variety of ways: using examples, words, graphs,
and equations. In two years, when they come to an abstract or dull
lesson in their high school algebra texts, I wanted them to be able
to think, "Oh yeah, I remember, like the toy car going down the
ramp."

Second, I wanted the students to recognize $f(x)$ notation as a
fancy way of describing the "in and out machine" games we'd
played in class, and to experiment with writing and graphing $f(x)$
equations of their own devising, being certain to review and include operations we'd learned with integers, exponents, and fractions.

FIGURE 4–3. *Pinocchio's Nose*

To chart his data in an easier way, we are going to re-name how many lies he tells to X, and how long his nose grows in inches to y.

how many lies he tells X	y how long his nose grows in inches
1	2 inches
2	4 inches
3	6 inches
4	8 inches
6	10 inches

this function table ← charts all the information so that you can see how things change

Can you predict how long Pinocchio's nose will be, after he has told 8 lies?

In the function chart we call X the independent variable, because Pinocchio himself controls how many lies he tells. We also call y the dependent variable, because his nose wouldn't grow at all if no lies had been told. So, in other words X has an effect on what happens to Y. In this case, Y gets 2 inches bigger every time X effects it.

FIGURE 4–4. *Pinocchio's Nose*

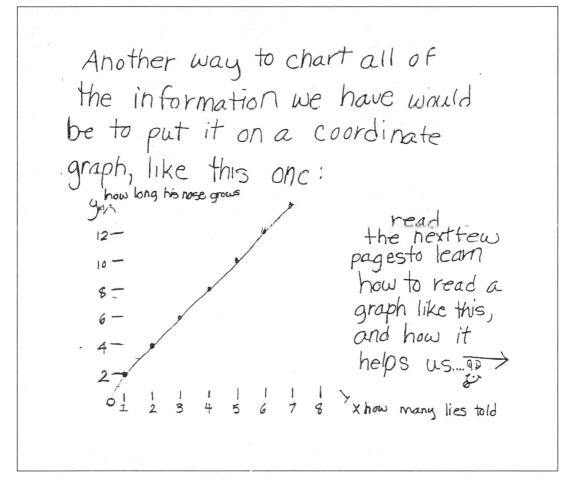

Finally, I wanted them to recognize the mathematics in real-world events in their lives. The children's book project was intended to allow me to assess whether students had indeed made such a connection. I thought that by becoming authors of math books themselves, they would further reinforce their vocabulary and understandings.

But even as I planned the culminating activity, a familiar debate raged in my head, one that I had not resolved by the end of the unit. The debate began as the tension between teaching such large concepts as functions and teaching more fundamental topics that would be covered on "gatekeeper" standardized tests in April and mid-May: basic operations in whole numbers, fractions, decimal fractions, percents, and integers, and some measurement and geometry concepts. These tests were important. One was the Algebra Readiness Test, a district gatekeeper for algebra classes consisting of multiple-choice responses to problems involving primarily fractions and percent concepts and manipulations. A second, more troubling one was the California Testing of Basic Skills (CTBS). Because of falling sixth-grade math scores at Horace Mann over the past few years, the CTBS was high-stakes not only for the students but also for the school because of its implications for district funding and staffing levels. I had worried that until the students could handle with facility the topics covered by these tests, the unit would be discouraging for me to teach and for them to learn. This worry kept me from introducing the functions unit until late in the school year, after I'd "taught the basics." I didn't make this decision lightly. Most of the students I was teaching at the time, at Horace Mann Middle School in San Francisco, came to me with very shaky preparations in basic operations. Few of my students— fewer than 10 percent, regardless of elementary school attended— have fluency with basic math facts in addition, subtraction, multiplication, and division when they enter my seventh-grade classes. They have trouble articulating the relationships between whole and parts, including division and fractions, and what they do know they do not connect to the mathematics of division and fraction algorithms, representations, and operations. Similarly, most do not control measurement in any dimension, including time. I find it difficult to separate this fundamental command of mathematics from conceptual mathematical thinking. I believe it is important for a child to make sense of 5×3 by knowing that this arithmetic phrase may be represented by five rows of three items each. But I also believe it is fairly useless for students to own that concept unless they can *also* rattle off $5 \times 3 = 15$ in three seconds. There is simply not time, when solving problems, to rederive every basic concept by counting.

Evaluation and Reflection

The timing of the unit certainly had an impact on my ability to evaluate its effectiveness. When the functional relationships unit finally happened, it was interrupted by the three-day seventh-grade camping trip, the inevitable end-of-the-year assemblies, and a school carnival. We had a total of six class sessions to spend on the unit, amounting to eight hours. Students were revising and submitting work up to the last day of school and some final projects were simply lost in the shuffle. In a locker or under a bed somewhere is an insightful delightful book on the functional relations in a Quinceañera (a coming-of-age ceremony in Latino culture that is roughly equivalent to a "sweet sixteen" celebration), and a well-written action-adventure science fiction comic book called "The Adventures of Dr. Math." I believe most students came away from the unit with a bit of confidence about dealing with algebra, and with something concrete they could recall when faced with the formalisms of high school math classes. Students had chosen to look at the ordinary events of their lives—birthday parties, allowance, cartoons, and even cookies—in terms of functions. As we struggled along, all I could think of was Jon Scieszka and Lane Smith's new book, *Math Curse*,[4] which shows the lunatic results when a child begins compulsively investigating everything in her world in math terms. I wondered where the authors had gotten their inspiration. It was our seminar run wild, working all too well, spawning a nightmare of maniacal adolescent math fanatics throughout the country.

But the math curse didn't catch on universally. There were students who floundered and failed. Because I continue stubbornly to be more than a little skeptical of ivory-tower incursions into my work-a-day teaching world, I had insisted at our initial curriculum seminar meeting that as part of keeping our work on functions "student-centered," each seminar participant should choose a "focus student" around whom to design a unit. I chose Loida, about whom I wrote:

> Loida is a personable girl who chats amicably during most class sessions when she attends school. She missed a month of school this year, as she has most years, to return to her

home country, Nicaragua. Her mother, who was a teacher in Nicaragua, works as a chambermaid here. She would like to return to teaching but does not feel confident of her English. She also seems not to realize fully that Loida is working at a fourth-grade level in math, although recently she has begun helping Loida with her math homework and therefore Loida has begun completing homework assignments.

In some ways, Loida is typical of Horace Mann students. The school is in the heart of the Mission District, San Francisco's oldest nonnative settlement and now a predominately immigrant Latino and Asian neighborhood. Horace Mann attracts students from all over San Francisco but has a large percentage of Latino students because of its location. Depending on the year, between 50 and 75 percent of the students receive Aid to Families with Dependent Children (AFDC), and about 70 percent have English as their second language. Horace Mann was restructured as a bilingual magnet school in the mid-1980s, as part of an out-of-court settlement of an NAACP suit to integrate schools and raise academic standards, particularly for students of color.

How did my focus student, Loida, respond to the unit? Very disappointingly. I attributed her lack of results to burnout; she had made excellent progress earlier in the year and did not have the energy to sustain her work level to the final days of June. At that time I wrote:

> Loida made visible progress during the year, going from the 25th to the 50th percentile on the CTBS standardized math test (the students take only the "Concepts and Applications" portion of the exam and *not* the computation section). Her class grade improved from a D– to a C–; during the last part of the second quarter and throughout the third quarter she voluntarily came to lunchtime tutoring lab at least four times a week as well as working at home with her mother to achieve this improvement. Her willingness to attempt work in class and her note-taking skills improved as well as her math computation.

Loida attributes her change in study habits to the fact that

during her month in Nicaragua this year, the friends she had
had in San Francisco, mostly girls with fringe affiliations with
Latina gangs, formed other friendships and excluded her
when she returned. She was a loner for a while and then
began to work with a group of girls who were quiet in class,
non-Latina, and rather weak students. Interestingly, her
former friends also made dramatic gains—greater than 30
percentile points—in skills and test scores, supported either
by parents or tutoring programs in organizations such as
Youth in Action and Mission YWCA and by discussion
groups organized by the social services director at Horace
Mann.

On the final unit on functional relations, Loida and her
partners completed the activities diligently, but their
homework and write-ups were disappointing. Her group of
four splintered. Two girls completed a project that completely
missed the point. Loida and her partner had ambitious plans
to do a book and audiotape, then a videotape, but finally
completed, and submitted, no final project. I believe that
although Loida had made gains during the year, the quality
of her understanding is still shaky, and too shaky to absorb
the new concepts. I think she was intimidated and confused
by the language of the unit, and, having put so much effort
into the previous two quarters, burned out. During the three
weeks of the unit (the last three weeks of school), she stopped
coming to lunchtime tutoring, appearing only once for help
with the "create and graph your own functions" assignment,
and her tired teacher did not insist. Her mother, who
expressed how pleased she was by Loida's improvement in
class and on the CTBS tests, relaxed her support as well. It
would be interesting to be able to follow Loida's progress in
eighth grade to see how much of her seventh-grade gains she
is able to preserve and build on.

In fact, Loida's eighth-grade teacher, who offers little outreach
or outside-of-class support to students, moved her to a resource
special education class. When he learned from me that she had

scored in the 50th percentile on the standardized tests, he commented, "But that's high!" and expressed surprise that she had done so poorly in his class. Her resource special ed teacher, Gia Okebello, a capable and dedicated teacher, reports that Loida is recovering concepts and learning new ones much more rapidly than the other students and retains her conscientious attitude and study habits.

Loida's fate keeps in front of me not only the tension between skills and concepts but the huge challenge of teaching mathematical concepts well. Students with a much stronger math foundation struggled with several elements of the project: predicting; understanding how functional relationships relate to other math topics and other types of relationships; and using graphs of functional relationships to predict results for which we have no observed data. This identified areas in which I need more grounding in order to be able to guide students more clearly.

Intermezzo: How Sean Caught the Math Curse

The following year, I changed schools and concentrated my work in the area of language arts. But I took the functions unit with me, handing it on to my colleague, Sean Donahoe. Handing it on, in fact, provided a good test of how well the ideas could travel and adjust to different teachers, styles, and students.

Our current school, Rooftop Alternative School, has a very different cultural climate from Horace Mann. Although it is also a San Francisco public school, it first became an alternative school decades ago, when admission was on a first-come, first-admitted basis. Parents camped out, sometimes for days, to gain entrance for their children. This process favored more affluent families. In our present class, fewer than 5 percent of the students receive AFDC, and while about 10 percent are bilingual immigrants, all the parents are middle class and speak English. A few years ago, the process changed to admit by lottery after favoring siblings of present students, but the students we teach now belong to the last class to gain admission by the "parents camping out" system. Subsequent classes will have a more diverse census.

Rooftop had been a K–5 school, but the parents and principal elected to expand to K–8. Sean and I are the first seventh-grade teachers; we have sixty students whom we divide into two classes. We do not believe in tracking, and, as at Horace Mann, the classes have students of mixed strengths. In fact, the one thing that makes our team teaching coherent is the shared conviction that all students can achieve to high standards if given the opportunity to explore curriculum through engaging projects and to grow by reflecting on what and how they learn.

Sean's Tale: Implementation

I taught the unit beginning in mid-January, making changes as needed. I agreed with Amy that many hands-on activities help kids develop a feel for functions and the accompanying vocabulary, but I used science activities rather than her "toy stations" for several reasons. First, I was comfortable with the science activities from teaching them in previous years. Second, I perceived that understanding the math functions could enhance the students' understanding of the science.

For an opening activity, we investigated the number of paper clips an increasing number of magnets could attract and hold (see Figure 4–5). The activity is ideal because of the surprises it contains—an opportunity to wrestle with the ideas of prediction and varying rates of change. Looking at the student work, it is clear that these surprises are thought-provoking. The students predicted that the number of paper clips that could be carried would increase constantly with the number of magnets employed, and were surprised by the diminishing returns. As students used the "t-tables," patterns became clearer to them. They began internalizing which variable was the *choice* variable (independent) and which was the *outcome* variable (dependent).

Few kids used graphs spontaneously. Trying to teach graphing skills at this point was challenging—next time I would start graphing right away. I liked the data-recording document Amy had used, but I thought the space to write conclusions was inadequate. Next time I will add a third page to the recording form to enable the students to do three things: first, discuss what skills they have

FIGURE 4–5. *Student Work on Magnets*

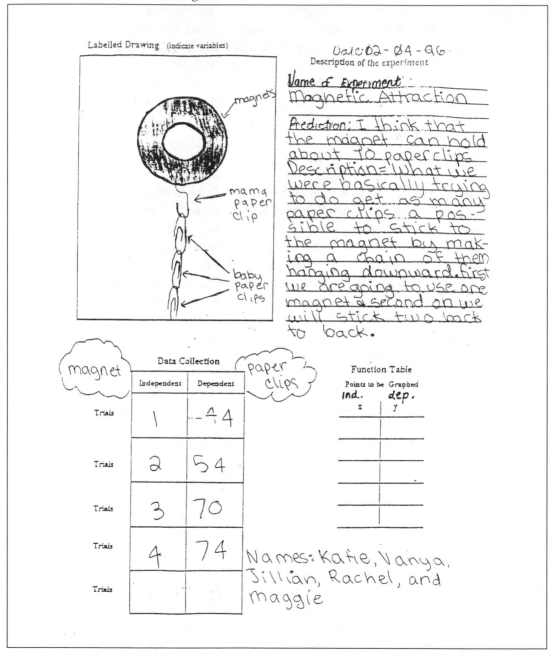

FIGURE 4–5. *Continued*

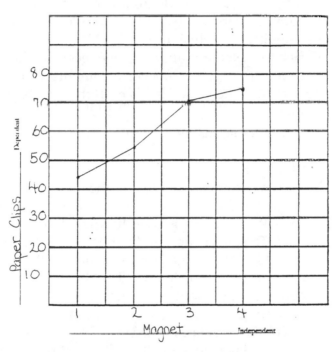

Title Magnetic Attraction

Can You Draw What is Going to Occur

Conclusions

The more magnets there are, the more paperclips are able to be held. One other conclusion our group made was that the number of paperclips didn't dramatically increase because the magnets were busy holding themselves together.

gained from this activity; second, restate the hypothesis and conclusion; and third, correct their conclusion so that, ultimately, their papers have scientific accuracy. In this way they can become more aware of their successes as learners, refine their abilities to make hypotheses, and come away with scientific knowledge they can relate to the challenges of their lab work. I field tested this modification of the "extended conclusions" in a writing exercise I had them do following the magnet activity called "Magnetic Personality." For example, in Rebecca's "Magnetic Personality" conclusions she is able to make reasonable predictions based on the relationship she sees. She chooses to rerepresent her data in a t-table and her comments and notes demonstrate how clearly she understands both the events and their representations:

Magnetic Personality

by Rebecca Johnson

P1: Experiment

We were attempting to find the magnetic force that each magnet had and how it was able to magnetize the paper clips. We were trying to see how much mass the magnets can hold. The paper clip could not be between two magnets and it could not be hanging from the hole in the middle of the magnet. The magnet(s) could not be resting on any surface, it had to be suspended in the air.

P2: Actual

This is the data collected.

# of magnets collected	# of paper clips
1	21
3	21
1	41
2	23
4	18

I thought it would be the more magnets you have, the more paper clips will hold. Now from the data I have collected I see that the more magnets you have the less paper clips are going to hold.

In her prediction, Rebecca also provides a possible scientific explanation for the data:

> If we were to have 10 magnets I think that there wouldn't be very many paper clips sticking. I think this because based on the results I am thinking that if you put the magnets together the more you have, the more stick together. So it kind of backfires because the magnetic force is too busy having so many magnets stick together it does not have enough energy to hold all the paper clips you hang there.

Garrett, on the other hand, becomes confused when the data are inconsistent with his expectations. He writes:

> Different numbers of magnets totally effect [*sic*] the number of paper clips that are picked up. With one magnet we got nineteen to thirty-six paper clips. With two magnets the number of paper clips almost doubled, our number was fifty-three, but we had some answers that were a little bit higher. Three magnets I didn't understand because we got thirty-six again.

In his "What if?" section Garrett concludes:

> What if we had ten magnets? Our results would be in the hundreds. I think that ten magnets could hold just a little more than 250 paper clips, because of our results with two magnets. I determined this number by multiplying the number of clips on two magnets by five.

Eva's group checked their data but remained puzzled. While unable to provide a "commonsense" prediction, Eva is still able to use her data to generate a consistent prediction.

> When we did the experiment, we had to very carefully hook the paper clips onto the hook, so as not to upset and/or add energy to the experiment. For one magnet, Lia and I were able to place 23 paper clips on the "S" before they fell. For two, 39 paper clips, for three, 50 paper clips. The strange thing about this experiment was when we tried four magnets

we could only hang 49 paper clips. We tried this a few times, always with the same result.

What if there were *ten* magnets? Well, it's hard to say. With our results, who can know except by trying? My guess is that it would stay the same number or we would be able to get more paper clips on. This is based on my general knowledge and common sense. However, based on my results, I would have to say that the number of paper clips would lessen, even though that goes against all common sense.

Later, I had the students do the bottle activity shared at the curriculum seminars by Ron Ritchhart.[5] I sketched data plotted into curves on the board and then I asked the students to describe vessels. Rachel captured the bottle function well using a qualitative narrative (see Figure 4–6). The relationship was clearly represented without reference to numbers and specific quantities.

I then added an element by showing the students the vessels so they could analyze their successes and mistakes. Students' approaches and levels of success ranged widely. Some drawings showed an understanding of a constant versus variable rate of change. Other students were able to see the connection between the shape of the bottle and the graph but were not yet able to properly indicate the direction of the cause-and-effect relationship. Shantia's paper (Figure 4–7) provides a wonderful diagnostic tool for modifying teaching to address an area some students were struggling with: she clearly connects the graph to the physical features of the bottle, but talks of the "decline" of the line rather than an incline, indicating that she may be reading the graph from top to bottom rather than from left to right.

My biggest source of satisfaction was in revisiting with students lessons I had taught in September. With their new experience with functions and graphs, the lessons became much more meaningful. The district science curriculum emphasizes cycles: weather patterns of coastal and valley cities, temperatures, sunrise, sunset, tilt of earth. In the past, I have always had kids tabulate the hours of sunrise and sunset, measure the flagpole's shadow over time, and look at temperatures in eight cities (coastal versus central valley

FIGURE 4 6. *Rachel's Data Sheet*

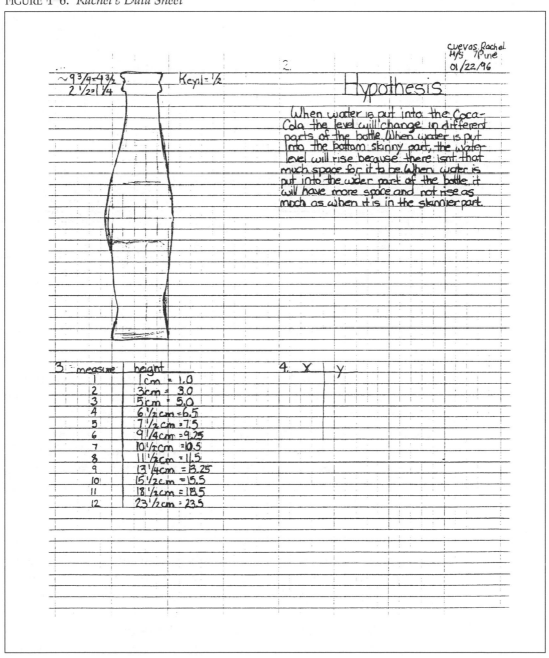

The handwritten data sheet contains:

Cuevas Rachel
4/5 7 une
01/22/96

~9 3/4 ~ 4 3/2
2 1/2 = 1/4   Kcyl = 1/2   2.

Hypothesis

When water is put into the Coca-Cola the level will change in different parts of the bottle. When water is put into the bottom skinny part, the water level will rise because there isn't that much space for it to be. When water is put into the wider part of the bottle, it will have more space and not rise as much as when it is in the skinnier part.

3. measure	height
1	1cm = 1.0
2	3cm = 3.0
3	5cm = 5.0
4	6 1/2 cm = 6.5
5	7 1/2 cm = 7.5
6	9 1/4 cm = 9.25
7	10 1/2 cm = 10.5
8	11 1/2 cm = 11.5
9	13 1/4 cm = 13.25
10	15 1/2 cm = 15.5
11	18 1/2 cm = 18.5
12	23 1/2 cm = 23.5

4. | X | Y |

FIGURE 4–7. *Shantia's Bottle Graph Analysis*

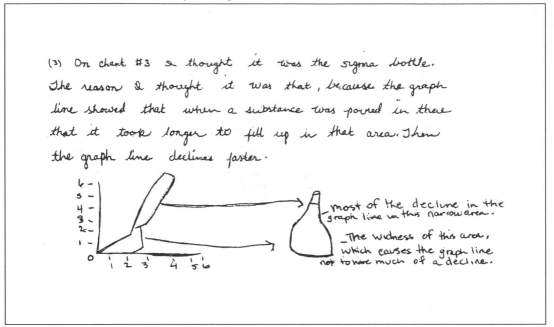

versus desert). By mid-October I would always be very frustrated. The kids wouldn't be able to determine what season it was when given just three days of data. But after the functions work, they began to graph the information, and they saw it. Now they seemed to understand why things change: they saw the change. We didn't actually come up with symbolic expressions for these relationships, but the students were now talking in terms of range, positive slope, negative slope, ascending, descending, even "sine curve," to describe the cycles of increasing and decreasing daylight. Eva, Rachel, Ben, Shantia, Carissa, and Neysa wanted to know if they could do extra cities! It was a huge breakthrough when Ben said, "So as the line goes up, the length of day is increasing; right? If the line is going down, nighttime is increasing, and the daytime is decreasing."

When we decided to once again end the unit by having students create their own children's books, it really helped to have the exemplar books from Amy's class the previous year. Students enjoyed looking at *Pinocchio's Nose* and *Graph Your Cupcakes*. While Amy had allowed the students to choose their groups, I structured the groups more. Since we had discussed how important the visuals were to capture the fifth graders' attention and hook them, I first had the students nominate or volunteer themselves as artists. The kids who volunteered usually were average or below academically, and knew they could excel as the designated artist/illustrator. Then I had each artist choose someone they wanted to work with. Finally, I allowed the other students to migrate to the groups they felt most comfortable with. Sure, friends hung together, but the arrangements provided for a mix with a different center, without the teacher passing judgment. It provided a reason and a need for the less-than-average student to rise to the occasion.

Groups began by brainstorming story lines, and eventually each settled, by elimination, upon one theme. To facilitate group process, I used pizza to model how to select from the brainstormed ideas. I put choices on the board: extra cheese, mushrooms, salami, bell peppers, and (mine) anchovies. We raised hands to select what we did *not* want. Anchovies lost immediately, having only my vote. Salami was eliminated because of the many vegetarians. Finally, mushrooms won! The process was quick and efficient, and it eliminated normal bickering and divisiveness.

I introduced and modeled storyboard concepts on the blackboard. These help the group make decisions about the selection of elements for the story and the placement of information, data, charts, and graphs. They also provide a structure that ensures a smooth flow from the beginning of the narrative to the data involved.

Despite all the modeling and processing, it became clear that some groups had concocted stories that were so detailed and outrageous that they could not be presented and explained by two-dimensional coordinate graphs. *The Wily Coyote* project initially included about five variables: dynamite, rope, ambulance, bandages, Acme supplies. So I made an extra effort to have each table's facilitator understand that the data chart and graph must reflect the *outcome* of *one choice*.

We continued using the pizza model to examine the complications associated with multiple variables. We generated a data chart to determine how many cups of mushrooms the mushroom slicer would have to slice. Students chose a standard of two cups of sliced mushrooms per pizza. But then some commotion broke out: what size pizzas? what about foccacia? deep dish or thin crust? It became evident to most students that an effective presentation would have to eliminate some variables. Hence, the independent variable, the number of pizzas, must have the size and type of pizza as a constant: there can be no mixing if the graph is to be correct and consistent for a variety of pizza sizes. What emerged was an understanding that became very important in the development of the booklet.

After a while, groups petitioned to have more than one graph, because they began to understand the task, enjoyed creating the stories, and really wanted to inject more fun into their project. We discussed this and came up with some negotiated resolutions:

1. Students could use several smaller charts and graphs to give multiple examples to the fifth graders, so readers could practice or experience more than one sample and be led more gently into the final data chart and coordinate graph.
2. At the end of the booklet, students could pose a second choice or variable for the story, then close with the *1001 Arabian Nights* concept of saving the new idea for another story, another day, another booklet—even something the fifth grader might try!
3. If the math is complicated, students could use it to arrive at a final concept. They needed to maintain the complexity of the story, but they could reduce the math for the functional relationship to a workable form.

Sean's Reflection

Some of the things that Amy found difficult came more easily to me as a science teacher; prediction, for example, was not a stumbling block. On the other hand, I found myself explicitly using vocabulary I hadn't used before in science class: distinguishing between dependent and independent variables, discussing ascendant and descendant curves, and steepness of slopes. Moreover, I had not anticipated the graphing problems students would encounter, like rationalizing intervals, labeling axes properly, and giving titles to the graphs.

We were pleased by the results from the second year of this unit. Although I spent about the same amount of time on the unit, the students had had enough previous experience with data collection that they seemed not to need as many initial activities to get the idea. It also helped to have the exemplars from the previous year.

Some of the booklets really reflected the school's cultural climate. Just as it might have been difficult for most of the Rooftop students to appreciate the booklet with the Quinceañera theme, we doubt many Horace Mann students could have related to the steeplechase theme of one of the Rooftop books:

> Misty's trainer decided that she needed a training track, measured to fit her strides comfortably. After watching and measuring and charting, he concluded that for every one-foot jump, Misty needed a twenty-five-foot start in order to clear it. For each foot higher, she needed an additional fifteen feet.

However, for the most part the booklets reflected interests common to seventh graders: cartoon characters; endangered species; fantasy stories like *Hippie D* and *Princess Liberty*, who gets magic beads added to a necklace in proportion to good deeds performed; or the *Peg-Leg Pirate of Termite Island* (see Figure 4–8), whose wooden leg is consumed by an infestation of termites. The farther he walks in search of treasure, the more leg he loses. The story opens as follows:

> Once upon a time there was a greedy pirate named Harvey. He was so greedy he cared about nothing much of common sense. His true goal in life was to become richer than any man alive even if it killed him in the process . . .

Students then go on to weave functions into the story as part of the narrative.

In reviewing students' work, we think the areas of struggle are the most instructive. For example, the issues related to graph

FIGURE 4–8. Peg-Leg *Story*

To show the amount of wooden leg left on Pirate Harvey, we show it in a graph called a coordinate graph. The two main lines that represent the graph is called the y axis and the x axis; the y axis a vertical line, and the x axis a horizontal line.

Here, the number of steps the pirate took to get to the treasure and back is the x axis and the length of the wooden leg is the y axis.

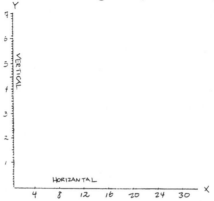

Label the x axis with numbers starting with zero, next four, and so on marking each label with the multiples of four. This is because for every four steps, the termites took a bite out of Harvey's' leg. The y axis should be labeled by whole numbers by ones. also, a coordinate graph should include a title, based on the title, and each coordinate graph has equal intervals to the x and y axis.

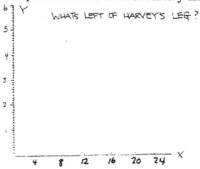

labeling—the graph of *Termite Island* is labeled "What's Left of Harvey's Leg" but, when completed as the authors direct, it will actually show "How Much of Harvey's Leg Has Been Consumed." Other books showed clearer labeling and sophisticated understanding of differentials, such as one called *Acres of Elephants*, an investigation of the relationship of elephant deaths to deforestation, a subject we had broached in social studies. Disconcertingly, this same group, while posing good questions in a quiz at the end, made a simple mathematical error in the answer key. That error masked another nuance of representing real-life problems with functional relationships. The graph showed that if five acres were cut down, seven and one-half elephants would die; while the graph shows a helpful relationship, in real life we would have to deal with discrete, not continuous, elephants.

We found another book, *The Story of Wily's Grueling Pain*, interesting because of its use of two types of graphs. The students chose a line graph to represent the functional relationship of the length of Wily's hospital stay to his costs—which they researched by phoning a hospital—and a bar graph to represent the progress of his bumps. To us this shows a glimmer of control over what mathematical tools best communicate different types of information.

In general, we worried that there was too much text relative to illustration to appeal to fifth graders, but this may be an issue we are inventing based on experiences at schools where the literacy levels are not so high. The students may be the best judges of what their younger siblings will be willing to read; we will find out next quarter when we field-test the booklets with the fifth graders. Overall, literary quality of the booklets was high, as an excerpt from *Termite Island* suggests:

> They sailed for many days and many nights. The days were hot and humid. The sun beat down on the crew. The ocean shimmered like gold as if the men had already found their treasure. . . .

Perhaps the fact that I told them they'd be getting language arts credit from Amy helped motivate the literary quality!

We agree on the usefulness of the unit. Graphing really aided the kids in understanding much of what they are learning in science. The data sheets, modified to include a reflection and correction page, are an effective tool. The books, which are a motivating project and a thinly disguised means for teaching someone else, require students to communicate and clarify ideas. As such, they are an effective assessment. The books underline some teacher roles as well. They require constant modeling of behavior, strategies, and samples, and the use of the identified vocabulary. Second, they require constant checking in with groups, querying them about status, level of understanding, and comprehensibility of story lines. In our minds, an assessment task that demands strong teaching pushes us in helpful ways.

Most centrally, we feel the project succeeds because students truly want to be able to put their math to work. If it works for them, they can understand it, even teach it to someone else. The unit will therefore remain a part of our curriculum. This may carry risks, as demonstrated by two students, Mike Weil and Graham Leininger, who started by looking for a functional relationship between time in class and the number of my puns, and now compulsively explore further refinements: the $f(x)$ of puns to raising class morale, to getting attention, or even to detracting from learning altogether, or the inverse, to demonstrating points. These students have clearly been infected with "the math curse."

Notes

1. The ideas for the toy functions activity and the worksheet students used to record their work came from Bayle Maggi's 1994 presentation on "Concrete Function Activities" to the Western Regional Math Conference, San Francisco, CA.
2. See Chapter 1 for a description of these activities and Appendix B for actual lesson plans.
3. Masaichiro Anno and Mitsumasa Anno. 1983. *Anno's Mysterious Multiplying Jar*. New York: Philomel Books.
   James Fey. 1971. *Long, Short, High, Low, Thin, Wide*. New York: Thomas Y. Crowell Publishers.

Leonard E. Fisher. 1982. *Number Art: Thirteen 123s from around the World*. New York: Four Winds Press.

Leonard E. Fisher. 1987. *Calendar Art: Thirteen Days, Weeks, Months, Years from around the World*. New York: Four Winds Press.

Robert. Froman. 1972. *Rubber Bands, Baseballs, and Doughnuts. A Book about Topology*. New York: Thomas Y. Crowell Publishers.

4. Jon Scieszka and Lane Smith. 1995. *Math Curse*. New York: Viking.

5. See Chapter 1 for a description of these activities and Appendix B for actual lesson plans.

Do Fish Sleep?

Using Functions to Guide Scientific Inquiry

Mike Benway and Ron Ritchhart

As a graduate student in biotechnology and biomedical sciences, I hadn't planned on becoming a teacher when I was recruited ten years ago to teach and help design the science component of the Urban Scholars program directed by the University of Massachusetts at Boston. However, with my own disappointing experience as a student in the Boston public schools fresh in my mind, I embraced the opportunity to introduce urban students to my world as a research scientist and provide a form of educational enrichment, guidance, and mentoring that might ultimately see these kids into college. Yet, soon after I started, it became clear to me that my delivery of specific advanced facts, concepts, and ideas was not a meaningful entry point for these urban students, despite their "gifted and talented" label. The typical student entering the middle school Urban Scholars program has had an impoverished science education devoid of laboratory or experimental experiences. What instruction in science they do receive consists primarily of sparse and disconnected factual knowledge from out-of-date textbooks—information the students often consider irrelevant. It wasn't that my students couldn't learn the concepts or retain the information; it was more that they were having trouble grasping the content of science because they had no understanding of the process of science.

In helping students to understand the process of science, I have always tried to draw on what it is I do as a research scientist. This means a focus on the actual processes I go through in my work. When I can translate those processes into experiences with ordinary and accessible problems, I can help my students understand science and its power. Early on, this focus led the Urban Scholars program to adopt a science fair format for our instruction. The fair captures the essence of what research scientists do. In particular, the judging clearly stresses the most important fundamentals of good science: formulating clear questions of a well-defined scope, conducting good background research, devising and carrying out well-designed experiments, carefully collecting data, faithfully recording observations, effectively communicating results, and fluently discussing implications. Becoming involved in the PACE curriculum seminars provided me with a new perspective on what I do as a scientist; the emphasis on functional relationships was a way of further focusing my instruction.

Understanding What Scientists Do

I didn't need much convincing regarding the importance of mathematics in general and functions in particular in doing science. When I am grappling with a problem, I find myself unconsciously "graphing my way" through it. For example, a graph carved into the sand with my big toe while walking along the beach may represent my early exploration of the relationship between two variables. My initial hypothesis about a relationship between variables in a proposed experiment may find its first representation in a graph scribbled on the back of a napkin. After experimentation, the validity of my initial hypothesis is evaluated by a comparison of the graph constructed from actual data to that of my crude initial drawing, which may in turn lead me to speculate about the underlying nature of the experimental design or suggest the possible existence of other, as yet unsuspected, causative influences.

In my daily work, the tools of mathematics related to data collection and display are a tightly woven component of my scientific thinking. The graph is a central tool through the entire process, reducing all of the speculative functional relationships in research to a single malleable symbol. Because they are applicable to an infinite variety of phenomena, graphs are so enmeshed in my process of scientific thinking that it is difficult to imagine doing science without them. I don't know how one can share Darwin's "Malthusian insight" without first floating a succession of normal curves in some perceptual space. How can one have insights into sociology without appreciating the rules of mass action? A nearly perfect analogy for a nonscientist would be to try to imagine what it means to think without language. Can you think right now without some words in your mind? It may be conceivable, but the facility and sophistication brought to the process through the use of the basic tool of words may render this experimental activity unrecognizable.

I recently attended a conference on the biology of aging sponsored by the American Association of Clinical Chemists here in Boston. Switching hats from scientist to teacher, I momentarily detached from the proceedings to reflect on what was actually happening. What were these scientists doing? Here was a room full of people viewing a long and rapid series of graphs projected onto a screen at the front of the auditorium. Over a hundred graphs and tables had been shown in the course of the day. We looked at graphs of mortality versus age for men with and without prostatectomy, graphs showing the increase in incidence of focused versus diffuse breast cancers over the last few decades, graphs of bone density versus age for postmenopausal women with and without tamoxifen therapy, and so on. These graphs often reflected data on tens of thousands of subjects, huge studies collapsed into an instantly comprehensible form. Whenever the presenter spoke, it was generally to draw attention to particularly important details of the graphs. If I were from another planet and were told that these were scientists, my first take would be that scientists are people who make and discuss charts and graphs. True enough in this situation, but what is it that they make charts and graphs of? What are these graphs and charts about? Of course, the answer is relationships. Scientist explore relationships and produce charts and graphs to report their findings.

Math and Science, Science and Math

As a scientist, I know that math and science are deeply integrated and share a reciprocal arrangement. Isaac Newton is said to have invented calculus in order to assist him in understanding physics. Indeed, it is a common undergraduate lament that in order to understand physics one needs to understand calculus, but in order to understand calculus, one needs to understand physics. As a teacher, I also know that both math and science represent formal expressions of processes that are fundamentally natural and intuitive for humans. I would suggest that any student who can crumple up a failed math quiz, toss it in a perfect parabolic arch that takes into account wind resistance against the irregular surface of the rotating object, and land it neatly in a trash can sitting at the far corner of the classroom has more innate understanding of physics and calculus in her cerebellum than could be contained between the covers of any undergraduate physics or calculus text. In teaching, my task is to tap this vast resource of intuitive understanding and connect it to the formalisms of math and science.

My science instruction has always relied heavily on the integration of mathematical skills. Students actually take measurements, record observations, make graphs, and discuss results. In a typical session, two students might be standing on chairs holding a meter stick up to the ceiling lights while two other students learning to read a light meter call out data for a third group of students to record on the blackboard. Yet another group of students might be measuring the diameter of a balloon in successive stages of inflation while other students estimate the area of a rectangle drawn on the balloon's surface and prepare to plot the data. Eventually, the class would be pulled together for a more general discussion that emphasized relationships and connections between these graphs and the related phenomena.

The classroom scene was usually quite chaotic, somewhat haphazard, but never boring. Above all, the sense was that these sessions were successful. Something real happened in these classes. It was very unusual, a little hard to understand, but exciting. Had I been complacent, I might have stopped there in developing my instruction. After all, the students were happy, and they seemed to be learning. However, upon reflection I recognized that these labs relied heavily on my planning and directing the students' activities. In addition, they were almost always directed at discovering predetermined underlying principles. Although this was much more meaningful to students than learning the information from a textbook, I still wanted students to have the opportunity to really experience science by acting like scientists, designing their own investigations and experiments and carrying the scientific process through to completion.

This shift clearly was needed. A review of students' current science fair projects, completed at their schools rather than in the Urban Scholar's program revealed little understanding of what it means to do science and provide scientific evidence. Most of the projects students were producing were simple show-and-tell displays. Few of the students demonstrated an understanding of the process of questioning, experimenting, and communicating that I felt was so important in my work as a scientist. Furthermore, a review of the projects at the regional competition showed a marked difference between urban and suburban students. Not only did the suburban students have greater support and access to materials, they had a superior understanding of the scientific process. Our program might not be able to do much about materials, but we could certainly address students' understanding of the scientific process and help them in the innovative use of ordinary materials to answer more general kinds of research questions. This is where the PACE curriculum seminars fit in. By placing greater emphasis on the examination of functional relationships, I could help students begin to become problem finders, to think in more graphical and relational terms, and to use math as an important scientific tool not just for displaying data but for understanding and making sense of their findings.

Using Functions to Learn Science: Exploring a Simple Question

I wanted my students to experience the thrill of actually understanding something about the way the world works by deliberately gathering a tangible piece of information with their own hands. To create this opportunity, I began a line of inquiry with a simple enough question: "Do fish sleep?" The question is interesting yet nonthreatening. No one felt stupid for not knowing the answer. My students all had definite opinions and could reach no clear consensus on the answer. I began to probe further, "How do you know whether or not fish sleep? What is your evidence?"

"I have seen my fish sitting still at night," a student volunteered.

"Well, how do you prove that? I mean, have you actually sat up and observed the fish continually for an evening?"

It didn't take much to get students to begin questioning their beliefs as they faced critical issues of proof and evidence. Soon, students became interested in adding some authority to their opinions and were motivated to find an answer. I had them hooked—already they were acting like scientists in search of evidence. This was important to me because I wanted my students to see that science is personally empowering. The insights gained through a well-designed experiment defy the identity of the experimenter or the authority of anyone who might not like those insights. My students had a question; now they needed a research design to collect some data.

As a class, we agreed to use lack of activity as a proxy for sleep. To answer our question of whether or not fish sleep, we would examine the functional relationship between activity and time. We would set up an experiment that would allow us to closely observe one fish. A long period of inactivity would tell us the fish was asleep and the length of inactivity would tell how long it slept. The time of its inactivity would indicate whether the fish was a nocturnal or diurnal animal. Time would be easy to measure, but what about activity? We would need a method to continuously collect data on the activity of a fish in order to create a graph of activity over time and determine weather that activity displayed any kind of daily rhythm.

Eventually, we came around to the method of connecting a light meter to a computer. The actual details of this are relatively nontechnical, and many devices can be assembled in various configurations to accomplish it. As a class, we constructed a flow chart written in simple English to serve as the basic blueprint for programming the computer, a task I would later do myself. Once the program was written, we tested it out using a rubber fish and refined the program accordingly. We discussed what size aquarium to use and decided that a small vessel would increase our signal or the number of counts per minute.

Finally, we were ready. Our instruments were set to detect a change in light intensity at the meter beyond a certain threshold and record that occurrence by printing to a disk file: the date, hour, minute, meter reading before the event, meter reading after the event, and the difference between the two. Our goldfish was placed in the small aquarium and left to sleep or swim with a bright light continuously burning near by. The light would provide nice sharp shadows for our recording device to measure while keeping the experimental conditions constant. Our fish would have no clue about the time of day from natural light.

When the class returned a week later, we found that the disk we were using had become full after about 40 hours (360 KB) and the program had shut down. Even so, our file of data was too big to be analyzed using a spreadsheet. Fortunately, we were able to get a high-speed line printer at the university to simply print all of the data out on large 132-column fanfold computer paper, resulting in a stack of paper approximately 7 inches thick! While the students were impressed with the sheer bulk of the data, the thought of analyzing it was intimidating. However, the job turned out to be more space-consuming than time-consuming.

We found a long corridor in the university and laid the printout on the floor, all 150 feet of it. Students then walked along its length, drawing a magic marker line across the page at each hourly increment on the printout. From this initial cursory analysis, a great deal of information became apparent. Students recognized that a simple, direct linear relationship existed between the activity level of the goldfish and the number of entries on the computer printout. The number of entries in an hour could be measured indirectly by the length of paper used to record that activity or the number of paces needed to walk from one hour to the next. It was immediately obvious to all of the students that the amount of activity varied considerably from hour to hour. Moreover, students recognized that the longer segments (i.e., the most active hours) tended to occur consecutively, as did the shorter segments. Crawling along a physical map of our data, we gained a fully tactile representation of an abstract quantity, activity.

The next step was to make a table. In one column, the hour on the printout was recorded. In the next column, we recorded the length in meters of the associated segment on the printout, which was proportional to the activity level of the fish during that hour. The consolidation of all of this into a graph was the final task. This became much more than a rudimentary exercise in which the students participated to merely develop a skill. There was an actual sense of anticipation of the construction of this graph. All of the steps thus far culminated naturally in the making of the graph. The graph represented the single object into which we would deposit the accumulated knowledge of all of the previous stages. In the graph, we would see if our activity data matched our speculative predictions and how it compared to the data we had seen in the literature.

The graph had a distinct sinusoidal pattern to it, displaying the telltale up-and-down motion of a sine wave. In fact, it seemed as if our fish had distinct periods of decreased activity around the middle of the night and perked up in the morning to stay active for most of the day. Looking at the graph, students were totally committed to the faithfulness of the analogy between it and the behavior of a living animal. They were able to attach a meaningful narrative to the graph to bring it to life and infuse it with meaning. Most importantly, the evidence provided in the graph allowed students to commit to their explanatory theory of the phenomenon underlying their observations. The graph was evidence. It supported a scientific theory. It proved something.

Reflections

By learning to use functions to work as scientists, my students had come to understand the power in the words of the eminent philosopher of science Karl Popper, who said, "While differing widely in the little bits we know, we would all do well to remember that in our infinite ignorance we are equal." Popper's words speak to all learners and lead us to the exciting realization that education is not a task to be completed but a continual line of inquiry to be pursued. Popper's sentiment teaches us that no matter how little we know, who we are, what neighborhood we live in, how much money our parents have, what our schools look like, we potentially have access to the future discovery of some bit of knowledge, a knowledge based on the authority inherent in the scientific process and use of the tools of mathematics. This statement about the infinite quality of our ignorance represents a sense of boundless opportunity rather than futility toward learning.

Our experiment, born of a simple question, not only proved something about our fish, but it also proved something about the students themselves: their competence. They were right, and the appreciation of the meaning of the graph was clearly key to winning these goods. With a sense of possession and comprehension of the abstract relationship between data and phenomenon, the way was open to moving deeper. New questions began to pop up: How does the fish know what time it is if the light is always on? Maybe it is just goldfish who sleep, how do we know? I heard that sharks can't ever stop swimming, what about that?

The experiment might be over, but the learning has just begun.

6

A Conversation Among (Critical) Friends

Ron Ritchhart with Joan Boykoff Baron, Donna Foley, and Roy Gould

Through Mathematical Eyes is the second volume in the "Moving Middle Schools" series. The name of the series is no accident. It was carefully chosen to reflect our emphasis on promoting systemic change—the kind of change that affects both what and how teachers teach and students learn. With this ambitious goal in mind, the PACE curriculum seminars asked teachers to take curricular risks and reflect critically on their instruction as they developed and implemented innovative curriculum. From the outset, we set high standards for ourselves and agreed that we were only interested in developing quality curriculum as evidenced by high-caliber student work. Clever ideas and engaging activities were only as good as the student work they promoted. This standard of evidence set our course, framed our discussion, and kept us honest.

As teachers developed and taught their units over the two years of the seminar, they also collected samples of their students' work to be critiqued by their peers at our group meetings. In sharing that work and the inner workings of the classrooms that produced it, the PACE teachers laid themselves, and their students, open to criticism of the toughest kind—that which is informed by genuine knowledge of the domain and based upon experience in the classroom. In these reviews of student work, teachers were sometimes pleased when others saw glimmers of understanding they themselves had not identified. Sometimes they were disappointed when they realized that often even their strongest students failed to demonstrate the understanding that "seemed" to have been there.

Such public scrutiny is intense. It also provides one of our richest opportunities for growth as teachers if we can listen and try to answer the tough questions our colleagues pose. By forcing ourselves to give evidence of our students' understanding to colleagues, we avoid sentimentality, complacency, and mediocrity in our teaching.

By writing out the stories of their teaching, the teachers in this volume have taken their professional development one step further. They have actually spelled out both their successes and their struggles in planning, teaching, and assessing their units on functions. Along the way, they have shared examples of student work to provide an idea of just what it was their students did and to serve as evidence of their understanding.

In keeping with the curriculum seminars' emphasis on professional review and dialogue about our practice, this chapter documents a frank conversation about the hard work of teaching a complex concept like functions. The conversation brought together four educators. The first, Donna Foley, a middle school mathematics teacher and K–8 mathematics department chair in Chelmsford, Massachusetts, offers the insights of a fellow math teacher. As a scientist at the Harvard Center for Astrophysics, Roy Gould approaches the work from a practical perspective as a content area specialist. Finally, Joan Boykoff Baron, a consultant to the Connecticut State Department of Education and director of assessment systems at PACE, offers the perspective of an education reformer actively involved in the national standards movement. Ron Ritchhart, middle school math teacher, researcher, and architect of the functions curriculum seminar, facilitates the conversation.

We hope this conversation will find its place in the rich exchange of ideas—past, present and future—that must be a part of school reform if it is to be substantial and sustained. So, as you read, consider your own impressions of the classroom stories you read and the student work you examined; juxtapose your perceptions with those of the four forum participants; join in.

RON RITCHHART: Thank you all for coming this morning, and agreeing to act as critical friends to help look at this work sharply. To begin our conversation, from your various perspectives as a teacher, as a scientist, and as someone involved in education reform; what is it that really stands out in this work for you? What are the things that you really value?

Donna, you represent a teacher's voice and that of someone not previously associated with the project. Consequently, you bring a new perspective and a different angle from which to look at the teachers' work. What struck you as you read through these chapters?

DONNA FOLEY: First of all, I really appreciated the way the functions were broken down to an appropriate level. Typically, when you first start to study functions you are in maybe a second-year algebra course. Before that, you'll work with money or equations and such, but you really never look at them as representations of functions. You see them as only linear equations, graphs, or quadratics but never look at the relationships between them. It was nice to see this all broken down into steps that younger students can take. And they were interesting, accessible steps.

Another thing that I liked about these teachers' instruction was its activity base. The students were actually performing the experiments. Also, the math wasn't in a little bubble "out there" as an isolated topic. The units all emphasized real relationships, and consequently, the students appeared to have a vested interest in what was going on. Even weak students appeared to get into the problems. They may not have followed through or given final results, but at least there was active learning going on by the students. I also appreciated the fact that these were real teachers working in real classrooms with real students. There were students in each of the classes who didn't follow through and do the homework assignment, yet when it came down to them participating in the activity there was still a lot of learning going on.

Recently I have come to value students being able to communicate and make mathematical connections, and these units showed evidence of that. Students had that opportunity to make some connections to the real world that you don't necessarily find in textbooks or in standard workbook activities. Even when textbooks do provide such activities, I know that sometimes teachers may tend to read them instead of do them. I liked the fact that in these classrooms the students were *doing*.

RON RITCHHART: Roy and Joan, both of you were here at the very beginning of this project and had the chance to see this work in an embryonic form. Now that you've had a chance to look at how teachers built curriculum based on those experiences, what are your overall impressions?

ROY GOULD: What I find especially valuable is the overarching approach, the idea of taking an experimental approach or a discovery approach to functions. It's incredibly valuable for several reasons. First, it starts to blur the distinction between science and math and between student and investigator. It also makes things exciting for both the teachers and the students. Perhaps the most important thing you can do in a classroom is to first get the teacher excited, and I think there's clear evidence of that in all of the classrooms. The third thing is that it is an absolutely open-ended approach. By putting the *nature* of experimenting into the hands of the students and teachers, you don't constrain at all what can come up in the investigations. Whatever is important to the students and teachers is naturally going to come out. I think that's the best path to developing activities that are likely to have an impact on the classroom.

JOAN BARON: There are two other things I see going on here. There is the "big-picture" mathematics—the idea of functional relationships. But there is also the small mathematics, which is contained in the numbers and operations that instantiate these relationships. They're both important. That partnership is really what I think this book is about. If we approach the units from both of those standpoints, I think we have an important way to look at the strengths of each of them.

And yet, each one of them needs to have both the problem-finding, big-picture mathematics *and* the small-end mathematical precision in measuring, calculating, and graphing.

RON RITCHHART: Does that relate to what you were talking about, Donna, in terms of seeing mathematics beyond the bubble?

DONNA FOLEY: Well, for me, part of that big-picture view of mathematics involves learning to see a world of patterns and looking for connections. In the work of these teachers, they tried to do just that. Think about all the connections with science, when they actually used the mathematics of functions to understand certain natural phenomena: pendulums, magnets, lung capacity.

Another aspect of getting math out of the bubble or looking at the big picture is in developing visual images. So often we just expect kids to do the math without considering how important it is for them to have images to draw on. Mike Benway talked about how important images were to his thinking as a scientist, and I know they are to me, as a mathematician. But too often we don't give students a visual picture. In their work with functions, these teachers all engaged students in concrete work that the students could see. I'm thinking especially about the graphing of the bottle problem in Sean and Amy's unit. There was such a strong visual connection between the data they collected and organized into a graph and bottle. I think the process the teachers went through really helped students to make connections.

ROY GOULD: I have a colleague, Marvin Minsky, who argues that you only really understand something when you understand it in more than one way. If you agree with him, then I think you can see how powerful the teaching in these examples is. Students have graphical representations of relationships and tables, and they have the actual experiments as well. They're seeing the notion of functions in many different ways. I'm not even certain that it's critical that they be able to tie all these together simultaneously at this stage. But it is important that they be exposed to them.

JOAN BARON: After reading your introduction, Ron, and then thinking about the big-picture kinds of things these teachers were all doing, I am struck by the thought that mathematics can help one appreciate the universe. Think about the example of Galileo with the pendulums and the fact that the period of the swing is associated with the square root of the length. I never knew that before. It is like discovering the pi relationship—by actually deriving it experimentally, by measuring circles and objects in all sizes, it really is awesome. Suddenly, you understand that pi is not some arbitrary number that somebody just pulled out of a hat but it has some real-world meaning, that it's always there. And it's stunningly beautiful. But is this something that a seventh-grade kid is going to relate to? What are your experiences as teachers, Ron and Donna?

RON RITCHHART: If someone tells you what pi is, if you've been denied the opportunity of discovery, it's very unlikely you'll just find the beauty in it.

DONNA FOLEY: But even if you know something as a fact like pi, when you give it meaning through a series of investigations, you actually rediscover it. It can still be, "Oh, my God! That's what it really is." A sixth-grade teacher I work with just did that. Her class used string to measure cans and to measure diameters, and later she came up and said to me, "Wow! I never knew what pi was. I knew that we used 3.14, but I never realized that it was a ratio." She said, "I'm overwhelmed!"—somebody in her forties.

I think we would probably have more mathematicians if kids had more opportunities to make discoveries like this that do reveal the beauty and connectedness of mathematics. I think that functions provide a great opportunity for seeing the beauty of mathematics and making discoveries. In the case of science, some students might want to continue a lifelong pursuit of those relationships. Functions can be a real entry point for them. But, like you, Joan, I do wonder whether because I can get excited about it in my middle-aged years, is an eleven-year-old going to get excited?

RON RITCHHART: The philosopher of education, Israel Scheffler, talks about the "cognitive emotions," and one is the "joy of verification" or of understanding something. While our students may not always key into the beauty of mathematics, I think they really do experience that kind of joy of understanding.

JOAN BARON: The kinds of investigations that the teachers describe in this book would lead to those kinds of discoveries. So if we're going to agree in fact that they're exciting for children, then that's a very powerful reason for keeping on with this work of teaching functions to middle school students in this way.

ROY GOULD: I wanted to say a word for ugliness here, too. As a scientist, I think one thing that is extremely powerful about this project-based approach to teaching functions is that students have a chance to see data that are ugly, that is, data that don't fit, because that is one of the motivating reasons behind progress in science.

I'm thinking especially of the experiment in Sean and Amy's classroom where students were picking up paper clips with different numbers of magnets. At first they started to have a fairly straightforward relationship: the more magnets the more paper clips. Then, suddenly, they hit the wall and having more magnets didn't seem to do anything. That is the kind of discovery experience that challenges both through mathematical sense and through scientific sense. It gets students to start thinking about what it means, what a relationship is. Is it engraved in stone? Is it something that's a description? And that really is the beginning of real science. A scientist in the eighteenth century, Oersted, I think, said, "There are really two kinds of scientists. There are the ones that look for beauty by finding harmony in nature and then there are the ones who look for all the things that don't fit." And you really need both because the things that don't fit are the ones that lead to questioning. It's never too soon for students to see that there are things that just don't fit. Actually, there are lots of examples in the work these teachers did that show "not fitting"—the magnets, the pendulum, the ball bounce.

RON RITCHHART: Is your notion of ugliness the same as being able to expect surprise? Or to expect to be surprised as you work. Doesn't a scientist, or a mathematician, need that?

ROY GOULD: And not be discouraged by that. It's an opportunity, not a put-down, of what you've done with the first five magnets.

DONNA FOLEY: Right. In math, we typically have given problems that have easy solutions: factor this, solve this for x, everything comes out to be a nice easy number. Only later do you find out that very few equations are factorable. So why do we ask kids to spend two months learning to factor? If they find out early on that things are messy a lot of the time, then they will look for easier ways to solve them. They'll look for a function, they'll look for a rule, they'll look for something to help them out.

RON RITCHHART: That was a distinction that Amy Benedicty wanted her kids to grasp. She wanted her students to see that mathematical functions, these ones that come out nice and perfect like in the "U-Say, I-Say" kind of problems, represent a very small domain of functions. She wanted to be sure her kids understood that these mathematical functions weren't the whole of it. That there exists an entire world of functions beyond the classic mathematical ones.

JOAN BARON: I'd like to interject a very sobering story because it's something that both puzzles me and troubles me, and it is related to what we are talking about here. This week, I had the occasion to watch a group of high school kids using a graphing calculator to solve a wonderfully interesting problem about the trajectory of a baseball. I was really thrilled with what I was seeing. I thought to myself, This is really neat, because you can hear them verbalize, "Well, the thing gets wider, the thing gets narrower, it goes this way depending on . . ." However, a colleague who was with me thought it was very disappointing that here's an Algebra II class in May doing this discovery unit all through trial and error. The students didn't know that algebra could be useful to them. When my friend alerted me to this, I thought, Well that is too bad. And Roy, you triggered this with your Marvin Minsky example. Algebra is a tool that could allow us to solve the problem without the graphing calculator.

Use your algebra and you don't have to spend an hour discovering it on the graph.

Do you think that maybe in seventh grade our expectations are fairly low along the algebraic dimension?

RON RITCHHART: Before addressing that question, don't we first need to ask what constitutes algebra? For a long time our concept of what is and is not algebra has been locked into the idea of equations. Unless it's an equation and unless we are balancing equations and solving for x, then you're not doing algebra. The graphical representation that the students in your story, Joan, were working with, and that Donna and Roy were talking about, traditionally hasn't been emphasized in teaching functions or algebra, but it is something that all of these teachers employed extensively.

DONNA FOLEY: Yes, in the old days you would teach algebra by saying, "Let's solve this equation," you know, "the two trains are coming and . . ." But we need to take the traditional algebra and expand it to cover other areas and to make connections. Just think about the "U-Say, I-Say" activity that Betsy and Marcy did. That's algebraic—it's figuring out an algebraic expression. The students say a number and the teacher uses an algebraic expression to change the number. If the students think and figure out the pattern, they are, in fact, doing the algebra. They're coming up with an algebraic formula, and that's great.

I think these teachers were all trying to broaden the definition of algebra and help make connections by asking, "When do we use this algebra? Now that we've studied this basic concept or skill, how do we apply the skill?" I think that application is the key. If you can find a way for students to apply a concept, they'll have ownership of it. They'll want to know more. Especially if it's an engaging problem like your baseball example, Joan, or Mike Benway's problem of "Do fish sleep?" That is one thing I really see happening in these units. The teachers are using simple but interesting problems to hook kids and show them how algebra can be used.

But you are right, Joan, we do still want kids to develop some basic skills with algebra. It may just be that some of those basics are changing. For instance, I would call the types of things that the students in your example were doing as definitely algebraic. If they were manipulating the coefficient, they had to understand things about what happens when you do that. Do you use a negative coefficient? What's the magnitude of the coefficient? What's going to happen? All of that is algebra.

ROY GOULD: The idea of connecting algebra to rich problems is really important. It is the most difficult and critical part of this whole endeavor. If we want kids to really understand functions, we have to show them how powerful they are for gaining understanding about the world around us. Otherwise, what's the use?

In looking at these units on functions, I see the activities grouped in three areas. The first type is discovery activities, where you're doing some experiments or exploring some very basic relationships. The pizza example is one where there's nothing particularly profound about the nature of the relationships, you're just noting that there are relationships. And then the second type of activity is one where you're really using functions to get at problem solving. The banquet table problem is an example of this kind of activity where being able to use the functions and relationships starts to help you solve a problem that you really couldn't do in another way. The third type of activity is one where you're looking at relationships that suddenly start to have some external significance, like the pendulum experiment, where you're varying the length of the string. It's not a human force that's determining this relationship, it's really something from nature.

This last type has a special quality. Hopefully problems are simple and accessible, but they don't always turn out to be simple relationships. It's these kinds of questions that can really get kids excited about what functions can do. I think that is what Mike Benway was talking about, that joy of being able to use functions to prove something. I'd really like to see the units head in this direction, but maybe there's an important progression among these types of activities. And we shouldn't lose sight of the fact that some activities are just descriptive where as others are more oriented to problem solving.

RON RITCHHART: To what extent do you see these three types of activities as a progression, Roy?

ROY GOULD: Take Joan's example of the students exploring the trajectory of the baseball. There was this sort of divergent thinking going on as they manipulated the parabola. The students were looking at ways of stretching that parabola, and they weren't really worrying about formalizing it. Somehow, that kind of descriptive, exploratory activity seems to come first in my mind. But I'm not sure.

If you think about the pendulum activity, it is so simple to do that you can uncover a very simple but powerful relationship quickly. You suddenly see, "Oh, yes! One variable is the square of the other." It's a very simple, but very big discovery. The students and teachers may not know what to make of it. What does one make of it? Why is it that way? We don't know. But there's something about seeing regularity that's very nice. Seeing a function can actually open up new avenues for exploration, particularly in science. In Mike's problem of "Do fish sleep?" the function the students found opened up the whole area of circadian rhythms.

JOAN BARON: But I don't want to lose the math in the exploration. We can all agree on the strengths of these units that teachers developed. They are engaging. They're real-world applications. They involve data collection, pictorial representations of the data, and, ultimately, graphs. Now I'm just turning it over and asking, Is the mathematics also being brought into play—the traditional mathematics, the skill-based computational mathematics, the stuff we've all been exposed to and taught how to do? Is that brought into play *enough*? I'm sure these units could motivate that. Do we indeed find sufficient math, or is it ending prematurely? Are we staying with the fun stuff, thereby doing students a disservice? These students may have positive attitudes toward mathematics, but are they going to be able to open up doors in their future lives if they don't also have the insurance policy of strong algebraic skills?

RON RITCHHART: I'd like to throw something else out for consideration in regard to your example, Joan. Doesn't your story point out that merely having the tools isn't enough? Couldn't it be that the way the tools were presented in the traditional algebra class didn't lead kids to think of applying them in this situation? Maybe they are used to problems being set up one way and one way only, and so they can't do them any other way.

But you raise a good point, Joan, in terms of how this whole endeavor is going mathematically. Are we delving into the deep mathematics and science? Why don't we pursue that now? I'd like to ask you all to look into the student work. We haven't talked about it directly yet. The question I want to pose is where do we see evidence that the assignments provide for that kind of deep mathematical work? Where do we see it not going quite far enough?

DONNA FOLEY: One of the concerns I had was with students doing the storybooks to show their understanding. The math is taking a back seat to the eloquence of the story. In the *Pinocchio's Nose* story (Figures 4–3 and 4–4, pages 80–81) the students did show an understanding of functions, but it was only a simple linear function, not something that was beyond what we would expect a seventh grader to be able to do. Betsy and Marcy touched on exactly this point in their reflections. I think we have to ask: "Is the communication placed above the mathematics?" For example, recently I was working with a group on scoring performance tasks and we noticed that middle-school students were getting very high scores on pieces, but they were fourth- or sixth-grade pieces that eighth graders were doing. Sure, they could explain them, but the mathematics just wasn't there. So I would say that it is important to set up guidelines and clear criteria for the math and science you expect.

ROY GOULD: The student rolling the cars down the inclined plane and then doing a graph of it and the accompanying description (Figure 2–4, pages 43–44) suggested to me that there was understanding. But how do we know when students understand? One of the teachers, Betsy, was talking about it: "We wanted them to understand the dependency relationships." And while that is an appropriate goal, we really have to ask how we will know when students understand. In our science education department we've now decided that the only indicators of understanding are things that begin with "The student is able to . . . ." Because we suddenly realized we haven't a clue what students understand, and we are perennially disappointed when we try to probe just a little deeper. So, even though we want students to develop an intuitive understanding of functions to help them see the world, there's simply not a good way to test that. But if you say "able to" and then actually construct a list of things that students will be able to do: find solutions, analyze tables and graphs, represent relationships. Well, at least you have something to really work towards.

I'd also like to pick up on the issue that Donna raised about students' writing. I too feel that when you read students' descriptions or listen to their verbal descriptions it's wonderful; it's eloquent. But sometimes there's something not quite there. Maybe this is an obstacle that stood in the way of students' understanding, but I noticed that a couple of the students said they had difficulty in articulating what a function was. And I suddenly realized that maybe words are incredibly powerful and that we shouldn't be so reticent to talk about the definition of a function. One of the teachers said, "I didn't want to just start by saying, well, a function is a blank. I wanted them to have lots of experiences." But then if the kids come away feeling that they can't quite say to their friends, "A function is a blank" in one sentence, then something is lost. So, we have this strange situation where kids can describe their experiments fairly well, even eloquently, as Donna said, but then there's something about articulating that concept which we know is hard.

JOAN BARON: So, isn't it a matter of linking a definition with their experience? That is the important last link that shows the kid really gets it and understands that this definition that we started out with and the experiences we had fit in the same universe.

ROY GOULD: I agree.

RON RITCHHART: You know, Roy, I appreciate your bringing up this issue because it is a tension that I've felt. Where does the definition fit in? When I went up to Maine and interviewed students in the middle of the unit, I noticed they were having a hard time defining a function. And when I talked with Betsy and Marcy about it, it wasn't that the teachers or anyone was trying to hide the definition from them. It was "What kind of definition makes sense?" and "When does giving a definition lead to understanding?" or "When does it blunt understanding?"

ROY GOULD: So, maybe the problem is that no one of the definitions of functions or ways of looking at a function is satisfactory. Because the rule or function machine definition doesn't really motivate the learning of functions. The rule is pretty easy to understand: you put something in, you get something out, but it doesn't really tell you why I, as a student, should be learning it.

JOAN BARON: Going back to your distinction of the three different kinds of activities, Roy, maybe the definition of a function changes somewhat with each type of problem. In that first group of discovery activities, functions are basically just relationships. You're just noticing that there's a relationship between the knob on the toaster and the color of the toast, for example. So, that's the first step—just understanding relationships, right? As one thing changes, that other one changes. But you don't know the nature or the direction of the relationship. You only have this global sense of the relationship initially, but the mathematics moves you from a relationship to a function. Relationship plus math equals functions.

But aren't we really talking about what it means to *understand* a function? Take Marlon's work from Amy's classroom (Figure 4–2, page 77). Okay. Now to a nonmathematician, it looks like it has potential to show understanding. If a student can do *a* through *e* on this list, create at least seven functions and include five with at least one of each of these operations, then that's a pretty good coverage of the algebra that one would traditionally expect to find at this grade level. However, the more I looked, the more I had to ask myself: "Is this just a regurgitation?" Maybe the understanding of functions isn't necessarily as visible as I initially thought it was. So, tell me, is this activity a bad thing to do?

DONNA FOLEY: No, I think it has value. The students can take functions, substitute values, and create a table and then graph those values. However, I don't think it necessarily shows that the child understands what a function is, or even all that much about functions.

RON RITCHHART: Yes, I agree with you, Donna. There's nothing wrong with this and it provides kids with some valuable experience, but based on this I'm not willing to say that the assignment required an understanding of functions. One of Amy's big concerns was giving kids computational practice and this activity was a really effective way for her to do that. But in terms of what they really had to understand, they basically had to understand the concept of a variable and the concept of substitution. They didn't really have to understand anything about functions as long as they could just set up something, substitute a number, and perform an operation. But notice that Amy did have students make a table of values and graph those. So they were connecting representations. But it's easiest to start with that formal rule to generate a table of values and then graph those. If Marlon had started from either of the other representations, it would have been much harder and shown more understanding.

JOAN BARON: I think that's what we're striving for, isn't it, these multiple representations? It's being able to come in at any place and get to the other places, seeing that they are all sort of equivalent at one deep level, right?

RON RITCHHART: Yes, I think that is key.

DONNA FOLEY: But understanding also demands being able to interpret representations. That was done some with the bottle graphs in Sean and Amy's class. Betsy and Marcy talked about it a bit as well. But it's an area that could be pushed further. Student interpretation of graphs is always difficult. For example, getting students to understand that when you're doing linear graphs the slope has a definite effect. When students really get into graphs, understand graphing and different types of graphs, they should be able to take the graph and work back to an equation. This work of Marlon's is just taking the equation and working to the graph. So I think all of the different representations are valuable parts.

In looking at whether Marlon's work shows understanding, I would say, "No." But there's still value in doing something like this because the student is now taking it in at least one direction. I just don't have any evidence that Marlon can take it back. If the student were given a graph, could he tell you which equation it goes with? Does it have a slope that was greater than another graph? Can he explain this type of graph? Or, if he were given some of the bottle graphs, can he tell me the type of bottle it is? Those types of things would tell you that a student has a good understanding of how all of the pieces fit together.

JOAN BARON: What you are defining for me is true expertise. But, can we get that within the confines of the mathematics curriculum that tries to do so many different things in a given year or a given three years?

RON RITCHHART: I think we have to take a hard look at the current curriculum that does try to cover a lot of disjointed knowledge, skills, and facts. With that type of coverage instruction, knowledge winds up being so fragile that we end up coming back to it year after year. It's like we're building on sand. Every summer the tide comes in and sweeps it out because the instruction has no roots. But if we work for depth, then we're really building, adding layers onto previous years' instruction. That's one thing that I find exciting about the work that these teachers did. In no case did the teachers say, "This isn't a topic that's at my grade level. This comes later." The teachers in Maine even ran into some problems with high school teachers saying, "Well, if you teach functions, then what am I going to teach?" as if functions were just a topic that you cover and then that is it. But what these teachers are doing is molding a core and next year's teacher can build on that and build on and on.

If we go back to Marlon's work, one thing that strikes me about this activity is that this would be the way most people would approach functions. The difference would be most people would leave it at that. His work is potentially more powerful because it fits into a broader context of instruction.

But I would like to talk a little bit more about any work that you see that's strong mathematically or scientifically. We've talked about Marlon's piece, but what other things did you see that you think are examples of strong math or science or that are generally effective instructionally?

ROY GOULD: The respiratory activities from Carrie's unit, blowing up the balloons and so forth (Chapter 3). They were looking at respiratory capacity as a function of age and also as a function of smoking. I really liked that. Here again one does have to come to terms with data that don't quite fit.

RON RITCHHART: What do you think an activity like that gives kids?

ROY GOULD: Well, the activity obviously connects to something that's real to them. The word that comes to mind is "control." That they in a sense have control over a study. Mike talked about this issue in his teaching. It is that sense of empowerment and knowing that you have access to knowledge. Also, Carrie's study is fairly straightforward to do and fun because you're blowing up balloons. It is effective because it combines a lot—it combines student's sense of control, it combines data and their learning to handle data, and then having to draw conclusions.

JOAN BARON: I'm generally not very impressed with interdisciplinary units because I don't think they do justice to any one discipline. I often think you have to have a discipline to enter into a topic and develop understanding through or else you are left wondering, "What's happening here?" Like "Where is the science?" or "Where's the math?" But I think that Carrie's unit is actually a very good example of an interdisciplinary unit. In fact, in some respects it is an extraordinarily powerful example.

What I don't know is if it's sophisticated enough for the grade level. Students are certainly learning about data, experimentation, variables. All of that certainly lives here or could live here if the teacher wanted it to. The other thing the unit certainly does is deal with the issue of smoking with kids at a very impressionable age. Perhaps if kids actually do these experiments and see the tremendous disadvantage of smoking with regard to lung capacity, it will make more of a difference than just learning about all the associated diseases that they think they're invulnerable to at that age. So the unit's got a health component that is strong and convincing because you didn't just read about some study, you did it. The question still remains: "What do we see when we look at the student work?"

DONNA FOLEY: All of the things that you're saying, Joan, are what make the problem rich. But I want to see it extended more than it is. To realize all that interdisciplinary power, you have to push it. From the work that's here, I can't tell if the students can hypothesize. You know, somebody that plays a bassoon has to have a huge lung capacity in order to play an instrument like that. Does that override the effects of smoking?

RON RITCHHART: Much of what Carrie had kids do was group work, so we don't have much individual work. That brings up the question of what can you determine about an individual student's understanding from group work. I would have liked more student reflection on what they understood, the problems that they ran into in collecting data, and the unresolved issues. You know, "These are the things we still wonder about." I think that would have given me a better sense of what it was that kids understood. I know that since this was part of a nonsmoking unit, Carrie asked her students to write letters to try to encourage someone to stop smoking. However, looking at those letters, the kids relied on emotional appeals, not on the data. That was a potentially rich avenue. So it made me wonder, "How do we create the expectation that you have to use the data?"

JOAN BARON: Well, the group work does represent the collective understanding, but you're right, you can't tell about individual understanding. So maybe that's an area to strengthen.

RON RITCHHART: In looking at Carrie's unit on the respiratory system, one of the questions that I have is, How much do kids really understand about controlling variables? It's what Roy brought up earlier, it's about ugly data, messy data. This is a messy problem—there are many factors that influence lung capacity.

ROY GOULD: And some of the kids had predictions about that. They thought that smaller people with smaller lungs would breathe faster—they were bringing in many other kinds of variables. So there were lots of theories about what might be going on, what might be happening. But I think that's not a bad thing. However, it really puts the onus on a teacher to sort all that out as they go through the activity and to focus on what it is that the kids are trying to figure out.

RON RITCHHART: Right. A teacher who risks doing this type of activity needs to think about the issues of how you can set up an experiment and what things you can control, what things you can't control. And when you do get the data, there is also a real statistical issue of recognizing what the limitations are.

ROY GOULD: Yes. This is one of those experiments that's big risk, big gain—big potential gain. Because it's all in there, if you can get at it. The real purpose of it could actually be sort of epistemological: How do you know something is true? How do you know or find out something? So, you've learned about smoking and your lungs, not by standing on the street corner and tossing theories back and forth, but by actually doing some experiments. I think that's the number one lesson that teachers should keep coming back to.

On the other hand, if students get discouraged by the experiment itself and never get results, then they may say, "Well, what's the point of doing an experiment?" Scientists can never learn anything if the data don't show anything. That's a really important issue to handle so students don't go away feeling like science is useless.

JOAN BARON: Is that likely to happen, do you think? Is it so complicated that they're not going to see results?

ROY GOULD: It does happen. Data are not always conclusive. But in this instance, students did at least see a trend. Looking at the scatter plot, there was a sort of a dichotomy in the results with two distinct data clusters. I have to say, my colleagues and I did this same experiment and we had the same thoughts. So it's not just their experiment.

JOAN BARON: But isn't the issue, as you were saying, taking control? In a very deep sense, taking control and controlling. You're taking control of the problem finding by setting it up and then exercising appropriate controls.

RON RITCHHART: Yes. The other thing this brings up is how, as educators, we can be very nervous about leaving kids with questions. That somehow it's bad. In fact, I think it's very good. I think one of the reasons why kids are not persistent in solving problems is that we've set up the expectation over the years that there has to be one answer to everything and that you, the teacher, will provide it. So it's a very important thing from the scientific perspective to be able to deal with uncertainty and unanswered questions.

In wrapping up, I want to ask you about how this work with functions needs to be extended. In what directions does it need to be pushed?

ROY GOULD: I want to see kids more responsible for their own learning. There were two ways here that were very, very nice and could be built upon. One is the self-reflection through vehicles such as journals and the second is the teaching of others. Teaching younger kids is something that we have found is very powerful. You don't really understand something until you can tell it to someone else.

Another point is that we really need better ways to understand what it is that students are not getting. I don't just mean wrong answers on a particular exam or activity. But more. Where are the problems and the misconceptions? One of the things that science educators are really beginning to appreciate is that students don't come to class knowing no science. Kids know a lot, and most of it is completely wrong. So in science, students have very strongly held prior conceptions, and I'm wondering whether there are prior conceptions with functions as well. I want teachers asking what it is that students bring to class. That would be a valuable body of information to consider.

Finally, I want to mention something that's been bothering me a lot in science education and that is this issue of "the need to know." The one thing that struck me most in the entire book was this one student you wrote about, Ron, in your chapter on the development of understanding (Chapter 7) who complained, "Why do I need to know about Christopher Columbus?" I thought about this for a long time, and I thought, "Well, one answer is you don't need to know, but you do need to *want* to know." There's an old saying in German, "You can't want what you want." It seems that our task as educators is to expand what it is that our students want to know.

It's a huge undertaking, but obviously the kind of work these teachers are doing is the way to go. The discovery path taken here is the right one, but it really needs to be pushed further. One of the teachers said very eloquently, "Maybe it's that I have to concentrate on the purpose of this again." That's something that keeps coming back again and again. I know in science the big concepts like entropy and so forth are things that teachers struggle to teach. Yet when kids say, "Well, how will I ever use it," no one has a good explanation. The power of functions is that you have an answer. The real-world activities begin to address that question which will always lurk in the back of kids' minds: "Why are we doing this?"

7

In Praise of Messiness, Betting Against the Odds, and Reinventing the Wheel as Avenues for the Development of Understanding

Ron Ritchhart

Some may look skeptically at a reform-minded project centered on teachers' design of new curriculum. Curriculum design is a long and arduous process, and it can be difficult work in the best of hands. So why paddle upstream by asking already overburdened teachers to design curriculum in the first place? Besides, good materials can usually be found among the growing quantity of outside resources. Why reinvent the wheel? In reading this volume, you have reviewed the efforts of the teachers in the project, examined students' work, and participated vicariously in a conversation about the larger issues of standards, quality, and understanding surrounding this enterprise. In the process this question "What does curriculum writing really offer as a form of staff development for all of its messiness and challenges?" begins to loom large. To address this issue, this chapter examines where the work of curriculum design and development can take us and explores the larger lessons we can export to new settings. At the same time, the chapter looks back at our specific work with functions to analyze the process of developing these units and identify what we learned.

Curriculum Development as an Understanding Performance

For expediency and excellence alone, curriculum development might best be left in the hands of the experts. However, if we want to effect long-term classroom change, we should ensure a role for teachers in this endeavor. Curriculum writing offered the teachers in the seminars a powerful opportunity to develop an understanding not just of their subject area, but of what it means to really learn and understand a particular topic well. This deep understanding of a topic has the power to transform a teacher's immediate teaching practices in ways that no prepackaged curriculum can.

When teachers wrote their own function units, they had to grapple with their own understanding of functions. They had to examine their own misconceptions, seek out connections to other topics, look for applications outside mathematics, consider and compare various definitions of a function, explore alternative entry points into the topic, investigate the many possible representations of a function, and determine the core features of a function. Armed with their own rich understanding of functions, or any other topic, teachers approach teaching differently. Knowing why their topic is important and how it fits into the larger curriculum, teachers display more confidence. They are more sensitive to possible misunderstandings, flexible in their instruction, and inventive in their assignments. In contrast, prepackaged curriculum is intended to be "adopted"; the emphasis is on "implementation" and "delivery." Teacher understanding of key concepts is often a neglected component.

By contributing to the intellectual life of teachers, the development of deep understanding of a topic can have ripple effects far beyond the teaching of an immediate unit. Through intellectually stimulating curricular work, teachers forge new passions, acquire more confidence, and assume greater responsibility for the delivered curriculum. Thus they contribute to the intellectual ethos of a school—an ethos many educational reformers have described as a necessary precursor to the establishment of rich, intellectual environments for children.[1] Deborah Meier, the codirector of Central Park East Secondary School and author of *The Power of Their Ideas*, has written extensively about the importance of defending a rich intellectual life for teachers within the confines of schools, calling it an "obligation" of teachers and part of the "very adult strengths needed to be good teachers, wise adults, and carriers of professional status."[2]

The curriculum seminars built an intellectually stimulating climate for teachers by inviting teachers to, first and foremost, become learners themselves. Broad topics such as immersion journalism, culture, and functions, each having wide appeal and applicability, were chosen for study. No one was asked to bring their favorite lesson on the topic or to pull together a collection of resource materials, teachers simply came ready to learn. They approached the topic as learners first and teachers second. Of course, the understanding teachers developed in the process of designing their function units didn't just happen. Rich, deep, assumption-challenging understanding seldom does. To be sure, the teachers' understanding was carefully facilitated and nurtured along the way. Immersion in a set of rich, hands-on experiences such as the rice bottle function, the puddle activity, and a trip to the Science Museum, all of which were accompanied by ample reflection and discussion, was a crucial beginning step. (See Appendix B for more information on these activities.) We also relied on outside resources and knowledgeable experts such as Roy Gould, a scientist at the Harvard Center for Astrophysics, for both valuable expertise and an injection of confidence that we were indeed moving in the right direction.

As important as this initial learning experience was in generating excitement, curiosity, and a basic level of understanding, it wasn't until teachers embarked on the process of designing a curriculum that their understanding began to develop real depth. To do this effectively, we had to break old habits of curriculum development. Pulling together a collection of materials from various sources and merely picking and choosing an appealing set of activities was insufficient. We were looking to create experiences that mirrored our own immersions—ones that would facilitate and nurture a rich understanding of functions in our students. To help us in our endeavor four central questions guided our work:

- What expectations and assumptions of middle school students in general and our current students in particular need to be questioned?
- How can we challenge our current middle school curriculum to provide students with greater opportunities for meaningful learning?
- How can we teach in a way that engages and promotes understanding?
- What do we need to be looking for in students' work in order to adequately assess their understanding?

These questions were not initially articulated in our work but acted as unseen guiding forces. They emerged slowly as we began to recognize them as common themes in our conversations. These four questions have nothing to do with functions *per se* or even with standard issues of curriculum design, and that is the source of their power. They are about setting high standards, rocking the boat, and moving beyond the status quo. As such, they are readily transportable guides for anyone wishing to move their curriculum in a new direction. In retrospect, I wish these questions had been there at the beginning. We could have addressed them more directly, written about and discussed them openly, and used them to push our work further. Nonetheless, they serve now as a useful lens for reviewing and understanding the work that we did do. I leave it to those reading this book to better capitalize on the power these questions offer.

In the next sections, I explore how our focus on each of these four questions guided our overall work and helped us collectively develop a better understanding of functions. In doing so, I examine both where we have been and where the work needs to head next as it is picked up to be revised, expanded, and tested by others.

Questioning Our Expectations

I recently watched a daytime talk show about kids and gangs. As the conversation turned to the issue of school, one of the high school students on the panel became angry and described how useless school was to him. "They always teaching me the same thing about how Christopher Columbus discovered America. Why I need to know that for? How's that going to help me get a job? You tell me, why I need to learn that?" Like this panel of rebellious adolescents, the participants of the curriculum seminars also dug in their heels and asked us tough questions regarding our choice of functions as a suitable topic for their middle school students. At our second planning meeting, Amy Benedicty laid her concerns right on the table. She had an obligation to prepare her students and give them the tools to be successful in later classes. Many of her students struggled with basic computational skills and therefore lacked the prerequisites needed to understand functions. Others agreed. Functions is a difficult topic. Would students be willing to grapple with such difficult and challenging material or would they assume the stance of the student on the talk-show panel, angry and defiant about the demand to learn what he saw as a purely academic lesson?

While these issues are related to curriculum, they are also about the expectations we have of our students. Can we expect students to grapple with difficult concepts? Can we expect them to think mathematically when they are deficient in computational skills? Can we expect them to find higher-level mathematical topics engaging and ultimately relevant? These questions challenge many of the expectations on which our curricula are based. I believe that the student on the talk-show panel wasn't raging against academics; he was frustrated with the redundancy, triviality, disconnectedness, and nonsensical nature of his school's curriculum. Perhaps students do not so much expect everything to be relevant as they expect things to make sense. Perhaps low performance is not necessarily about low ability but a response to a curriculum that undermines and devalues one's thinking and insight.

It is not easy to sort out the underlying causes of such complicated issues. However, we do have to look beyond easy answers and consider some alternatives. Ultimately, that is what we chose to do in the curriculum seminars. We didn't pretend to have the solutions or the definitive answers, but we were willing to explore alternatives and question some long-held expectations. What might happen if we asked our students to struggle with the big, complicated idea of functions? What if we taught skills in a more contextual manner? What if we capitalized on relevance as an entry point to explore the concept of functions deeply? Our students might just surprise us with what they are willing to do and what they can understand.

Challenging the Curriculum

Questioning our expectations about what middle school students might be able to understand and what mathematical challenges they might be willing to take on forced us to take a hard look at the current math curriculum. To what extent did the present math curriculum provide students with the opportunity to respond to our revised expectations and meet high standards of performance? What new opportunities for meaningful learning might be made available to students in the curriculum?

What we found when we examined the curriculum will not surprise anyone familiar with middle school mathematics. In spite of ever-increasing demands for higher levels of mathematical literacy, our curriculum at the middle school level continues to hover between elementary arithmetic and formal, abstract algebra. From the outset, then, our work was set against the backdrop of a larger national reform agenda aimed at providing middle school students with a more powerful curriculum supporting mathematical literacy and preparing them for the future study of mathematics. In order to do this, we had to challenge a deeply entrenched curriculum built on traditional views of how to best prepare students for the study of algebra.

Our selection of functions as a topic was a major step in challenging the traditional curriculum. This selection was guided by three criteria proposed by John Thorpe for the selection of topics to be included in a "thinking curriculum": (1) intrinsic value to the real life of students, (2) pedagogical value in laying a foundation for future study, and (3) intrinsic excitement or beauty to be found in the topic.[3] Functions are intrinsically valuable; they help us better understand, model, and make decisions in a variety of situations while serving as an effective and efficient problem-solving and communication tool. Functions have pedagogical value on many fronts; they allow students to move from a concentration on performing operations on numbers to a concentration on relationships, which constitutes a move toward abstraction. In addition, an understanding of functions lays the groundwork for the study of calculus, physics, and chemistry; it can also enhance understanding in subjects as diverse as photography, athletic training, and nutrition. Much of the intrinsic beauty and excitement of functions lies in the real-world phenomena they are able to model. Technology provides another avenue for engaging curiosity. The use of graphing calculators, the "Game Boy of mathematics" as Betsy Berry refers to them, can be tremendously motivating and exciting.

The study of functions offers middle school students a more meaningful, powerful, and exciting bridge into the rich world of algebra than does the standard exercise of solving for an unknown found in traditional prealgebra texts. The power of mathematics lies in its unique ability to model situations, and functions are at the core of modeling. Thus the study of functions provides an avenue for seeing mathematics as much more than procedures. Functions have been described as the central unifying theme in the study of algebra, the very "soul" of mathematics, and a necessary component for any "real understanding and appreciation of mathematics."[4]

Having carefully selected our topic, there were still many individual obstacles to overcome as teachers faced a variety of curricular constraints. Teachers were not necessarily free to act as autonomous agents making large-scale revisions in their curriculum. They felt pressure from a variety of sources. For example, Carrie Wong felt a great deal of pressure to cover her mandated science curriculum dealing with the various systems of the human body. On the other hand, Amy Benedicty was concerned with preparing her students for a high-stakes algebra readiness test that would be used to track her students the following year. The fact that real algebraic work with functions was not the proper preparation for an "algebra readiness" test was a profound bit of irony. Still a different form of pressure came when Betsy Berry and Marcy

Converse were confronted by a concerned high school teacher who was worried about the implications for her curriculum if students "did functions" in middle school.

Addressing such constraints often required us to look at the curriculum differently, to move beyond seeing it as a collection of skills and facts to be covered. Carrie was able to see that functions could serve as an organizing framework for approaching the content she was required to teach in science. Functions represented a big idea that could help to infuse more meaning into her teaching and engage her students in doing science. Amy struggled to reconcile her commitment to provide her students a strong foundation in basic skills with her desire to introduce them to bigger ideas. Ultimately her teaching partner, Sean Donahoe, led the way by connecting science and math instruction and teaching skills in context. While functions provide rich connections to the sciences, they also connect easily to other topics in mathematics such as data collection, statistics, number operations, sets, coordinate graphing, formulas, variables, and inductive reasoning. In this way, functions can address many skills. As a math coordinator for the state of Maine, Betsy used the concern of the high school teacher who feared her curriculum was being usurped to explore how what Marcy did in seventh grade might be built upon in later years.

Analyzing Our Teaching to Promote Understanding

Deciding what to teach is not always as easy as it seems. Both individually and jointly the curriculum seminar participants grappled with their expectations of middle school students and made a commitment to challenge the curriculum by including the topic of functions, but what did we actually want to teach our students about functions? How could we teach functions to our students in a way that would be both meaningful and empowering mathematically? Functions are complex and multifaceted. What would our instruction need to include if we wanted to build a deep understanding?

Defining functions would appear to be a natural place to start.

However, definitions themselves tend to impart very little understanding to the uninitiated. They sometimes obscure more than they illuminate. By their very nature, dictionary definitions appear cold, hard and flat on the page. They lack the richness of the real-world concepts they are meant to represent. For example, take "justice," which *The American Heritage Dictionary* defines as "conformity to truth, fact, or sound reason." This definition gives us little understanding of how the concept is used, why it is such a powerful human ideal, or how one goes about identifying or finding justice in the world. This lack of clarity and meaningfulness is apparent in the definition of a function as well. In high school you may have been introduced to (and been mystified by) the definition of a function as a set of ordered pairs (x, y) in which each value of x is paired with exactly one value of y. Or you may have learned that a function expresses a rule of correspondence between two sets. Formal definitions such as these represent less a starting point for our understanding than an endpoint since they can only be fully understood in light of a much richer understanding of the concept itself.

In trying to help our students develop a well-rounded conception of functions in both math and science, we knew we would have to look beyond textbook definitions. We recognized that understanding functions is a multifaceted process and that students' comprehension would grow only through engagement in a series of varied and significant experiences that were connected to the real world. This meant that our teaching of functions needed to be rich and varied.

For our own conception of the various aspects or dimensions of functions, we have relied heavily on the work of others. Researchers in the area of functions have identified two broad perspectives students' understanding of functions takes: a process and an entity perspective.[5] These two perspectives make it clear that a function can be approached in more than one way and are therefore useful tools in designing balanced instruction.

The *process perspective* focuses on the rule aspect of functions, examining how a function is put together. The game "Guess My Rule" is a good example of approaching functions from a process perspective. In the game there is a output connected to an input by means of a rule. The goal of the game is to identify the *process* by which the input becomes the output and express it as a formula or a rule. "Function machine" activities also focus on the process or rule that defines the link between the x variable and the y variable. Students are asked to perform the operation specified by the function machine to produce a set of new outputs. Operating from a process perspective, students see functions as a verb or something you do. You carry out the operations specified by the rule to turn an input into an output.

In contrast, the *entity perspective* focuses on the function as an object in itself, treating it as a noun instead of a verb. For example, when we look at the graph of a function, we see a thing, a set relationship, that doesn't ask us to *do* anything. Rather than focusing on individual inputs, outputs, and a connecting rule, we focus on the whole. As an entity—a noun rather than a verb—a function has a set of attributes that define it.

We kept these two perspectives in mind as we designed our instruction, but we recognize that we have just scratched the surface in terms of fully appreciating their significance for our teaching.

Examining Students' Work for Evidence of Understanding

While the idea that functions have both a process and an entity perspective provided a useful general framework for organizing our instruction, we knew that a rich understanding of functions entailed a variety of other components. Our examination of students' work across the range of classrooms included in the project helped us identify five different aspects of understanding functions: identifying dependency relationships, expressing rules of correspondence, creating and connecting representations, identifying attributes of functions, and performing operations on functions. Cumulatively these aspects add to one's understanding of functions, they are not sequential in nature but have an overlapping and continuous quality about them. In designing the function units, each teacher wove together a variety of learning experiences to focus on these aspects in a unique fashion. For example, Carrie's work with the respiratory system focused a great deal on identifying dependency relationships and, to a lesser extent, on creating graphical representations. In contrast, Sean made the process of creating and connecting representations the central focus of his work and pulled in the identification of dependency relationships.

Although no teacher included all five aspects in his or her instruction, there is evidence of each in the student work generated. If we pool the collective experiences of these teachers, we can better see what these aspects actually look like. Moreover, we can begin to generalize about what types of assignments are most likely to give us this evidence. Such an examination is the important final step that moves the act of curriculum development into a reflective stage that explores essential assumptions about teaching and learning.

Identifying Dependency Relationships

In identifying *dependency relationships*, students normally begin by developing a qualitative narrative to express the relationship. This narrative captures the salient features of the relationship without necessarily making reference to specific quantities. In doing so, it captures the function as an entity rather than a process. In an informal discussion about functions, a group of seventh-grade boys from Sean and Amy's class produced a qualitative narrative to describe the speed of a bike as they rode it from their school through the streets of San Francisco to their homes:

> "Well, the school is at the top of the hill so you're going to really pick up speed fast."
>
> "Yeah, each block the bike will be going faster and faster unless something happens. Like, you would have to put on your brakes or turn or something."
>
> "But when you finally hit a flat stretch in the road you'll be traveling at more the same speed, kind of flat like, just the same. Your speed doesn't change as much unless you really decide to pedal hard."
>
> "You could be traveling at the same speed if you're going uphill, it just wouldn't be as fast. You have to keep pedaling or you'll just tip over."

Such qualitative narratives account for most of our thinking and talking about functional relationships and can serve as a natural entry point into the study of functions. Narratives capture the episodic and dynamic nature of functional relationships and present them as stories to be told. A lot of information can be captured and conveyed in a narrative, revealing a great deal about students' thinking. For example, embedded in the qualitative description of the bike perilously navigating the streets of San Francisco is the implicit notion of rates of change and a clear sense of dependency relationships. Throughout this discussion, the boys are able to treat the speed of the bike as an outcome variable dependent on some other factor. In addition to the steep slope of San Francisco's streets, the boys recognize that the speed of the bike could depend on other things such as braking or pedaling.

In Sean's class, students were asked to describe the functional relationship between the height of the water in a Coca-Cola bottle and the number of one-ounce cups of water poured into it. For her hypothesis, Rachel constructs a qualitative narrative to describe what she expects to happen to the water as the Coke bottle is filled. In her narrative, she talks about skinny and wide parts of the bottle and the rise of water without reference to exact quantities. As she performs the experiment, she collects data and organizes it into a t-table as a set of ordered pairs. Thus, she moves from the entity perspective of her qualitative narrative to a more process-oriented view, connecting inputs and outputs that will later be used to construct a large graph of the relationship (see Figure 4–6, page 93).

Expressing Rules of Correspondence

In expressing rules of correspondence, students develop a process perspective of functions by focusing on the transformation of quantities. Students may work from initial rules, using them to create outputs given specific inputs, or they may collect and analyze data trying to identify a rule. Although each of these activities builds a process perspective, the mental demands they place on students are quite different, as a look at student work reveals.

Amy's class followed up its work identifying dependency relationships in physical phenomena by creating function machines that stressed the process perspective of functions. Students wrote their own rules of correspondence and then used them to compute outcomes from various inputs. In Figure 4–2 (page 73) Marlon expresses his understanding of functions as a process when he writes, " '*f* of *x*' means 'were [*sic*] going to do something to the *x*.' " In working from a rule, Marlon makes use of his computational skills by substituting a value for *x* and then completing the computation.

It is also possible to reverse this process and identify rules of correspondence through the examination of data organized in a t-table. Betsy and Marcy's version of "Guess My Rule," called "U-Say, I-Say," shows the many ways students can express a rule or function in words. These descriptions, while verbal in nature, differ from the qualitative narratives previously mentioned in that they make use of specific quantitative information to describe the rule by which two events are connected. Thus, the verbal description is no longer episodic and can be easily translated into mathematical symbols, an important goal of expressing rules of correspondence.

The U-Say, I-Say game requires students to consider a host of information at once, examine it systematically, detect patterns and connect them to mathematical operations. As the game is played, students must analyze the data and look for patterns and regularities, such as "when the I-Say number increases by one, the U-Say number increases by two." These patterns must then be translated into mathematical operations, like "you must multiply each I-Say number by two." As additional patterns are identified, the rule may gradually be built up and eventually tested. If the rule does not work, it will be refined and tested once again in an iterative process.

Students may struggle to detect patterns or relationships when the data are not presented in an organized, sequential manner. Remember the chart that Betsy and Marcy used to organize the data (see page 00):

They used the random nature of this game to show students that organizing data can be very helpful in detecting patterns. Even then, some students may have difficulty connecting the vertical pattern they observe in the data table with a mathematical operation that defines the horizontal relationship between values. Working back and forth between creating and discovering rules can be helpful in this regard.

In addition to activities like these, students may simultaneously work to develop familiarity with and fluency in expressing rules of correspondence to describe the dependency relationships they are expressing in qualitative narratives and graphs. However, this is a gradual progression for many students, and not necessarily an easy or natural one at that. The process is complicated by the fact that many functional relationships derived from real-world experimental data cannot be expressed as a single, simple rule of correspondence.[6] Rachel's Coke bottle experiment produces a graph with many varying slopes or growth rates. Both regularity and discontinuity can be seen in the data showing the relationship between the height of a ball's bounce as a function of the height at which it is dropped.

In this context, the process of learning to express functions as rules of correspondence is facilitated by the investigation of highly regular data with a strong visual-spatial saliency. Betsy and Marcy provided us with a good example of what this can look like when they asked students to plan a wedding reception at the local Grange hall by making use of the available tables, which seat one person on a side. Working with one-inch-square tiles to represent the tables, students extended their work with triangular tables to determine the greatest number of people it is possible to seat using any number of connected-square tables. The tiles provided both a visual and physical connection to the data that students collected. In the act of placing tile tables together, students were able to see that only two new seats are provided by each new table, rather than the expected four, since two seats were lost as tables were pushed together. By considering the visual arrangement, it was also possible to see that as tables were added to the configuration there consistently remained two seats, one at either end of the banquet table, while the two new seats were added to the middle. Such observation facilitates students' expression of a rule or correspondence of formula to describe the relationship. Emily described the relationship between the number of tables and number of seats by explaining that "if you know how many tables you have, you can just multiply that number by two, because every table adds two new seats, then you have to add two more seats for the ends of the banquet table."

Creating and Connecting Representations

Throughout their work with functions, students are developing the ability to *create and connect various representations* of functions, including narratives, graphs, tables, and symbolic formulas. Working flexibly between these representations, students blend both the process and the entity perspectives, seeing the function as a whole and as a set of input and outputs. Through this work, students develop a richer conceptual understanding that allows them to discern the abstract concept of a function. They are able to grasp the notion that the function is not its representation but that the function *is* the relationship, a difficult and nuanced distinction. It is this relationship that may be represented in a variety of forms such as tables, graphs, symbolic formulas, verbal expressions, or narratives.

In creating and connecting representations, students use one representation to create another. They work from data tables to create graphs, from formulas to create tables, from formulas to create graphs, and vice versa, weaving together a web of connections. As students work back and forth between representations, they build connections between the phenomenon and its representation as well as between one representation and another. As teachers, we can structure assignments and instruction to highlight this ability. Amy and Sean did just that, using a recording sheet for their investigations that helped students make the connections.

The connection between phenomena and representation is demonstrated in the work of Sean's seventh-grade science class. (See Figure 4–6, page 93.) Having drawn a graph of the relationship between the height of water in a bottle and number of ounces of water poured into that bottle, students were asked to predict which of two bottles matched the graph. In this way, Sean moved his students beyond data collection and graphing skills to the formation of richer connections between graphs and events. As Dena's writing demonstrates, she has become more aware of the important features of a graph and how they relate to actual phenomena (see Figure 4–7, page 94). In her analysis of her mistaken prediction, Dena talks about her omission of the "break point" in her drawing, indicating that previously she had not seen this as an important feature of the graph. Her write-up also shows that she has begun to focus on constant versus variable rates of change and slope, using her own vocabulary to talk about "the up tilting line" (slope) and "equally going upward" (a constant rate of change) as important features of graphs.

As students work back and forth between multiple representations, they can make many connections—between the actual phenomena, the slope of the line on a graph, the rate of change seen in the data table, and the coefficient of x in the formula. Students can come to recognize that an irregular pattern in the data table will create discontinuities in its resultant graph and that complexity in graphs indicates complexity in the formula or formulae used to express the rule of correspondence. The richness of these connections allows students to see a graph when presented with a formula of a particular phenomenon, to view the information contained in a data table as meaningful, and to read a graph as a relationship between ordered pairs of data that capture the essence of a phenomenon.

Identifying Attributes of Functions

As students connect various representations of functions, they begin to pay attention to the *attributes of functions* and the way in which these attributes manifest themselves across representations. For example, students may recognize slope as an attribute of a graph and learn to quantify it as they analyze data tables and construct formulas. Over time, students learn to *see* slope in the data and formulas even when a graph is not present. In the "bottle function" explored in several classrooms, students developed intuitive notions of slope as evidenced in their descriptions of graphs as consisting of up-tilting lines, curved lines, steepness, straight lines, and flat lines. Although the teachers in the project did not believe that their students were ready to connect their intuitive notions to a more formal conception of slope, these experiences lay the groundwork for further development. Like slope, the notion of an intercept is also most salient when presented graphically; however, later on it too comes to be associated with tables and formulas.

In order to notice these attributes, students must view each function as an entity having a set of characteristics that define it. It is at this point that the formal definition of a function begins to make sense. Working with sets of ordered pairs in tables, plotting these pairs as points on a graph, and using equations to find a second value when the first is given are all important in developing a solid understanding of the definition of a function as a set of ordered pairs such that for every x there is one and only one corresponding y value. Before this crucial attribute is fully grasped, students' understanding of functions is likely to be incomplete and to contain many misconceptions. For example, students frequently assume that any graph of a continuous line is a function while a discontinuous graph is not. This misconception is not likely to hinder students' progress in dealing with functions from a process perspective, but it will impede their ability to treat functions as objects. (See Figure 7–1.)

Attention to the attributes of functions also leads students to the identification of prototypical types of functions. Through their graphing experiences, students come to readily identify linear functions as a group of functions all possessing the attribute of a constant rate of growth. Sari, from Betsy and Marcy's class, makes this observation in the conclusion of her "ramp height" investigation. (See Figure 2–4, pages 43–44.) Similarly, students come to recognize exponential functions, constant functions, or power functions as having special characteristics that can be seen not only in their graphs but in their equations and data tables. These shared characteristics cause us to lump them together in families or classes of functions.

Performing Operations on Functions
Performing operations on functions requires students to see the function as an entity that can be built on, subtracted from, variously manipulated, and thus transformed. For example, presented with a

FIGURE 7–1.

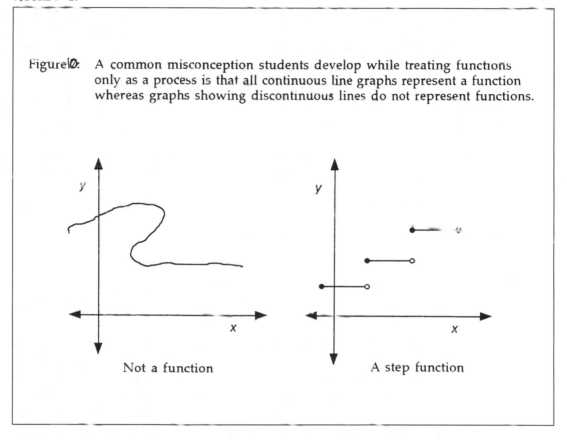

Figure 0. A common misconception students develop while treating functions only as a process is that all continuous line graphs represent a function whereas graphs showing discontinuous lines do not represent functions.

Not a function

A step function

linear function and its accompanying graph on a graphing calculator, students might be asked to create a second graph whose line is parallel to the first. To do so quickly and reasonably efficiently, the student must treat the equation of the first graph as a starting point and attempt to manipulate it through whatever operations seem reasonable. In this case, technology facilitates the manipulation of functions as entities.[7]

This ability to perform operations on functions enables us to transform the models we construct, using one function as the basis for a second. We can then consider the effects of those transformations.

FIGURE 7–2.

	A	B	C	D	E	F	G	H	I
1	Exch	Name	price	purchased	Total Cost	Share$Today	Current Price	Profit/Loss	% Gain
2	NA	ASSIXLNT	0.125	240,000	$30,000	0.53125	$127500	$97500	325%
3	NA	HITHWATCH	1	30,000	$30,000	1.125	$33750	$3750	12.5%
4	NA	FFOFNL	1	30,000	$30,000	1	$30000	$0	0.0%
5	NY	AMREP	5	30,000	$150,000	7.125	$213750	$63750	42.5%
6									
7	Formulas				.=C9*D9		.=F9*D9	.=G9-E9	.=H9/E9
8									
9									
10									

This is common in accounting situations. For example, filling out our 1040 tax forms takes us through a series of embedded functions. "Adjusted Gross Income" is a function of various predetermined parameters that is then used as the basis for a second function, our "Tax Owed." Within each of these functions are smaller, embedded functions. In constructing a spreadsheet to keep track of their progress in the "Stock Market Game" (Figure 7–2), Ashford and Mike from a Denver classroom used the function they created to find the total cost of a stock, column E, as the basis for the function of profit/loss, column H. This function was in turn used in constructing the function of the percentage gain, column I.

The five aspects of understanding functions identified here, in conjunction with the two perspectives on functions, provide a useful lens for both analyzing student work and organizing instruction. However, since this framework developed throughout the course of our work, we have not yet been able to fully exploit its potential for both planning and assessment. This is one of the important insights we carrying with us into our next round of revision. We gladly share them with colleagues as they undertake the design and implementation of their own units.

Conclusion

A quality curriculum must be more than a set of readily applicable skills. It must buy us a framework from which to make sense of the world and our place in it. Rather than being a strictly utilitarian endeavor involving the imparting of a collection of skills and knowledge, schooling can serve to broaden the scope of our vision, make new ways of thinking more accessible to us, and open up new avenues for our exploration. As students are exposed to these new ways of examining the world, they are able to consider the questions: Is this an area for me? Do I have a place here? Good education keeps those questions open, deferring closure for as long as possible.

Developing this kind of curriculum is hard, messy work. At times it feels like we are paddling upstream, struggling to keep pace with all the demands of teaching. However, the payoff lies in the possibility of changing lives. Involving teachers in meaningful curriculum writing changes the life of the school by fostering a learning community. It changes the lives of teachers by adding to their personal understanding of the disciplines they teach as well as an understanding of themselves as learners. And finally, it changes the lives of students as teachers help them build understanding by engaging them passionately and provocatively in powerful units about which they care deeply.

Notes

1. Seymour Sarason. 1982. *The Culture of Schools and the Problem of Change* (Boston: Allyn and Bacon).
2. Deborah Meier. 1996. *The Power of Their Ideas* (Boston: Beacon Press), p. 126.
3. J. Thorpe. 1989. "Algebra: What Should We Teach and How Should We Teach It?," in S. Wagner and C. Kieran, eds. *Research Issues in the Learning and Teaching of Algebra* (Hillsdale, N.J.: Erlbaum), pp. 11–24.
4. See Beslich (1928) and Klein (1904) as cited in Cooney and Wilson (1993), "Teachers Thinking About Functions: Historical and

Research Perspectives," in T. Romberg, E. Fennema, and T. Carpenter, eds., *Integrating Research on the Graphical Representations of Functions*, (Hillsdale, N.J.: Erlbaum), pp. 1–9.

5. See the following for examples of this research:

J. Moschkovich, A. Schoenfeld, and A. Arcavi. 1993. "Aspects of Understanding; On Multiple Perspectives and Representations of Linear Relations and Connections Among Them." In T. Romberg, E. Fennema, and T. Carpenter, eds., *Integrating Research on the Graphical Representations of Functions*, (Hillsdale, N.J.: Erlbaum), pp. 69–100.

J. Schwartz and M. Yerushalmy. 1992. "Getting Students to Function in and With Algebra," in G. Harel and E. Dubinsky, eds., *The Concept of Function: Aspects of Epistemology and Pedagogy*, MAA Notes, vol. 25 (Washington, D.C.: Mathematical Association of America), pp. 261–289.

A. Sfard. 1992. "Operational Origins of Mathematical Objects and the Quandary of Reification—The Case of Function," in Harel and Dubinsky, cited above, pp. 59–84.

6. A common misconception shared by students and adults alike is that a function must be a single rule. This is not a necessary condition, however. A function can be represented by a series of rules, each corresponding to a different aspect of the function. The step function is a good example of this (see Figure 7–1).

7. In addition to the graphing calculator, there is a growing amount of software that facilitates the manipulation of functions as entities. Examples include: the *Function Supposer* and the *Function Analyzer* by J. Schwartz, M. Yerushalmy, and Education Development Center Pleasantville, NY: published by Sunburst Communications.

Appendixes

Appendix A: Curriculum Seminar Schedule

Day One: Exploring Functions

Morning

Modeling the Process: Eyedropper Puddles
1. Recognize functional relationships
2. Develop language to describe functional relationships
3. Investigate functional relationships: model the process of data collection and organization using graphs and tables
4. Refine our description: construct a mathematical model in the form of symbolic formulas

Engaging in the Process: Exploring the Bottle Function
1. Practice processes 1–4 above through the bottle function activity
2. Predict the shape of data from the event
3. Predict the event by looking at the shape of the data
4. Explore beginning notions of rates and slopes by looking at the graphs of the data

Afternoon

Increasing Power and Flexibility: Incorporating Technology
1. Introduce graphing calculators; become familiar with the graphing and data operations

2. Construct a class database of various body measurements
3. Hypothesize and test correlational relationships and discuss the difference between functions and correlations
4. Construct mathematical models in the form of symbolic formulas

Searching for Functional Relationships: A Visit to the Science Museum
1. Identify functional relationships in the science museum; use language to describe them
2. Describe functional relationships with graphs
3. Describe functional relationships mathematically

Day Two: Developing a Unit

Morning

Identifying Core Themes
1. What did we learn yesterday? What are the key elements and features of functions?
2. What do we want students to understand about functions? Where do we place our emphasis?
3. Where's the math? the science? Where are the connections?

Scaffolding: How Do We Support Students' Learning of Functions?
1. What are the different points of entry?
2. What skills are necessary as a foundation? What skills are enhanced and practiced? Where are the extensions?
3. What structures and experiences are important? How do we allow for the gradual release of authority to allow students to become more self-directed?

Afternoon

Looking at Performances
1. What does understanding look like?
2. How will students work and what types of work will they produce?
3. What criteria can we develop for products?

Examining Materials, Units, and Resources
1. What's available to work with and build from?
2. What's strong? How can commercial activities and units be improved? How can they be incorporated?
3. How to incorporate the graphing calculator into instruction on functions

Day Three: Next Steps

Morning

Coming Up With a Plan
1. Work time with support to develop a personal or team agenda
2. Sharing of tentative plans, questions, and concerns with the group

Puddles Activity

Time
30–40 minutes

Materials
Plexiglas sheet (approximately 8 inches square), overhead projector, spaghetti noodle, colored water, eyedropper, grid paper transparency, centimeter ruler or overhead transparency of a centimeter ruler

Purpose
1. To provide an accessible entry point that promotes a discussion of the important features of functions
2. To provide a context for the introduction of vocabulary and the modeling of procedures related to data collection, organization, and graphing

Description of the Activity
Focus prompt
Students are told that they will watch a simple event taking place and will later be asked to describe and analyze the event. Discuss briefly the difference between description and analysis.

Demonstration

Place a clear sheet of Plexiglas on the overhead projector. Using an eyedropper, slowly drop one single droplet of colored water at a time onto the Plexiglas, allowing each drop to fall at approximately the same spot. Allow 8–10 drops to fall.

Discussion

Ask students to first describe in writing what they saw happening in as much detail as possible and then share their thoughts with a neighbor and jointly try to analyze the event. Ask several students to share their explanations and analysis with the class. Focus on aspects of their description and analysis that indicate a recognition of change, cause and effect, and connections. Introduce the vocabulary of independent and dependent variables and function.[1] A sample dialogue might progress along the following lines:

T: You said that the puddle got bigger, but it didn't just get bigger on its own, what made it get bigger? What did it depend on to make it bigger?

S: The number of drops you let fall.

T: So we can say that the size of the puddle depends on the number of drops dropped from the eyedropper. Puddle size is dependent on the number of drops. Puddle size is related to or is a function of the number of drops. Is the number of drops dropped from the eyedropper affected by the puddle size? No, so we can say the number of drops is independent of the puddle size.

To further emphasize the relationship between the variables, write on the board:

Puddle Size	is controlled by is affected by is a result of is *dependent* on is a *function* of	Number of Drops

Number of Drops   is not controlled by   Puddle Size
                   is not affected by
                   is not a result of
                   is *independent* of
                   is not a *function* of

Modeling
Now that the class has identified the independent and dependent variables, ask how we might actually investigate the effect the number of drops has on puddle size. What data would we need to collect and how? Incorporating students' ideas, form puddles of 1, 2, 3, 4, etc., drops of water on the Plexiglas sheet, then measure and record their diameters. The Plexiglas sheet allows you to pick up the puddles and measure their diameters from below without disturbing them. A transparency of a ruler marked off in millimeters (sixteenths of an inch will also work) may be placed under the Plexiglas and easily manipulated so that everyone can see the measurement taking place. Construct a table as follows:

Number of Drops	Diameter of Puddle in millimeters (or 16ths of an Inch)
1	4.0
2	5.0
3	6.0
4	6.5
5	7.0
6	7.5
7	8.0

Discussion
Discuss the relationships and patterns that emerge from the data in the table. Can you tell what is happening to the puddle from the table? A third column labeled "Growth" may be added to show a relationship that may be noted:

Number of Drops	Diameter of Puddle in Millimeters (or 16ths of an Inch)	Growth
1	4.0	
2	5.0	1.0
3	6.0	1.0
4	6.5	0.5
5	7.0	0.5
6	7.5	0.5
7	8.0	0.5

What can you say about the growth that is produced from each drop of water?

Modeling
Although we can see the growth of the diameter of the puddles in numbers, sometimes this relationship is easier to see in the form of a graph. Discuss what type of graph might be appropriate to represent the data. This provides an opportunity to clarify the differences between different types of graphs.[2]

Construct a scatter plot to draw students' attention to the fact that our data are grouped in pairs. For each and every number of water drops, there is only one size of puddle created. This is an attribute of a function: it consists of a set of coordinate pairs. Convention places the independent variable on the *x* axis and the dependent variable on the *y* axis. Connect the dots of the scatter plot, emphasizing that these are not our actual data but only a way of showing the relationship between the points and possibly what would happen if we were able to drop less than a whole drop of water. Again, discuss the relationship and highlight how the graph shows growth.

Looking at both the graph and the table, ask students to discuss with a partner and to make predictions for puddles of various sizes. Discuss how they are coming up with their predictions. Drawing on this discussion, demonstrate creating a *line of best fit* using an uncooked spaghetti noodle as the line. On the overhead transparency the spaghetti noodle can be easily manipulated to fit the data.

Assessment
Have students write in their journals how they would explain the concept of independent and dependent variables to someone else without using the example from class.

The Bottle Function Activity[3]

Time
60–75 minutes

Materials
An assortment of different shaped bottles or glasses of approximately equal volume. One bottle per student is optimal if time permits; one bottle per two students also works well. For each group of two students you will need graph paper, rulers, 8–16 ounces of rice (or water) in a container, a funnel, and a small measuring cup, scoop, or tablespoon.

Purpose
1. To use graphs and tables as tools to explore and analyze a functional relationship
2. To develop criteria for the analysis of a functional relationship
3. To develop skill in reading and interpreting graphs and connecting them with the phenomena they describe
4. To develop skill in predicting the shape of a graph from knowledge of the phenomena
5. To practice old and develop new vocabulary associated with functional relationships (independent, dependent, function, growth, slope, rate of change, linear, nonlinear)

Description of the Activity
Focus prompt
At the front of the room fill a clear glass bottle one scoop at a time with rice or water. Ask the class to watch what you are doing and

to see if they can identify a functional relationship between an independent and a dependent variable.

Discussion
In the discussion make sure that everyone is clear about the functional relationship and the independent and dependent variables involved in filling up the rice bottle. While students may notice more than one functional relationship, this activity focuses on the height of the rice in the bottle as a function of the number of scoops of rice added to the container. Ask students how we might further explore the effect that adding a scoop of rice has on the height of the rice in the container. As a class, devise an investigative plan that makes the investigative process, including data collection, and data-organization, clear. This process might be recorded on chart paper for future reference.

Activity
Students work in pairs. One fills a bottle with rice scoop by scoop and measures the height of the rice from the top of the table. (This means that for bottles with stems the subsequent graph will not begin at the origin.) The other student records and organizes the measurements. When all the data have been collected, the students work together to create a graph from the data. Depending on students' experience with coordinate graphing, this work may need to be supported. However, keep in mind that it is useful to get students' misconceptions and misunderstandings about graphing out in the open to deal with them effectively. Don't be afraid to allow students to make graphs with some errors. These will provide fertile ground for discussion later.

If time permits, students may switch roles and repeat the process on another bottle. When all of the graphs are complete, hang them up on a bulletin board and place the bottles randomly on a table below them.

Discussion
Ask students to look at the various graphs and see if they can match a particular bottle to a graph. This may be conducted as a

class discussion or students can be asked to record their answers on a sheet of paper with a written explanation. Ask students to provide explanations and reasoning for the connections they are making. In this discussion draw out concepts of slope, steepness, increase, and decrease. Emphasize specific connections between features of the bottle and those of the graph. As fruitful discussion diminishes, ask the makers of the graph to identify their bottle. Repeat this procedure until all bottles and graphs have been matched or leave some for another day.

Assessment

Show a new bottle, one that no one has used, and ask students working in pairs or individually to draw a graphical prediction of what the bottle function will look like for that particular bottle. After they have made their graphical prediction, have partners pair up with another group and explain the reasoning behind their graph.

Developing Criteria

The rice bottle activity provides an opportunity to begin to develop criteria for the identification of functional relationships. Explain to students that they have been involved in analyzing relationships both verbally and on paper, individually and as a group. Discuss and record the types of activities that made up the class' examination of the bottle function. This might include the following:

A Good Analysis of a Relationship Would . . .
1. State what the relationship is and identify the independent and dependent variables.
2. Be based on data from the results of an experiment that proves the relationship.
3. Include a graph and table that displays the data and shows the relationship.
4. Include a written explanation that connects the features of the graph with the actual event and includes descriptive vocabulary such as slope, rate, steepness, change, increase, decrease, linear, curvilinear, growth, and decay.

The criteria should be posted in the room and added to as new criteria emerge, so that they may be referred to during later sessions.

Self-Assessment
Ask students to review their activities during the class period and rate themselves on each of the established criteria. Which ones do they feel they (1) can carry out independently, (2) can do with the help of a partner, or (3) need more experience and practice with which to develop confidence?

Notes

1. Students frequently become confused between independent and dependent variables when they are presented merely as labels. This is easy to do since the independent variable is the one that is manipulated and controlled (dependent on our actions) while the dependent variable is left alone (independent of our actions). By using the words *independent* and *dependent* to state relationships rather than just as labels, some of this confusion may be avoided.

2. Students are generally most familiar and comfortable with bar graphs and may feel these are appropriate to represent these data. It is important to clarify that bar graphs are frequency distributions based on categorical data. They are used for answering the question, "How many in each category?" Students are somewhat familiar with line graphs from the stock market and weather reports. These graphs represent continuous data in which every point on the line has meaning. However, students may be less familiar with scatter plots. A scatter plot is similar to a line graph but only actual points have meaning. The points may be connected to indicate the relationship and as an interpolation based on the data.

3. A variation of this activity appears in the NCTM Addenda Series booklet, *Patterns and Functions* by Elizabeth Phillips. 1991. Reston, VA: National Council of Teachers of Mathematics. pp. 60–63.

Appendix C: Unit Lesson Plans

Unit Plan #1: (Chapter 2: The Mount View Story)
Betsy Berry and Marcy Converse

Note: From January 2-25, students met for a double block (105 min.) every other day. From January 25 on, students met every day for a regular block (55 min.).

Day 1, January 2
1. Collaborative Learning Community Contract (45 min.)
2. Grange Hall Problem (triangles and hexagons) (60 min.)
3. Homework: Tile Layer's Problem

Day 2, January 4
1. Collaborative Learning Community Contract (30 min.)
2. Bottle Function, Part 1 (straight bottles) (75 min.)
3. Homework: Pages in a Book

Day 3, January 8
1. Water Drop introduction on overhead (30 min.)
2. Bottle Function, Part 2 (curved bottles) (75 min.)
3. Homework: Self-Assessment #1

Day 4, January 10
1. Arm Span vs. Height introduction (40 min.)
2. Web Community Builder (20 min.)
3. Rumor Problem (45 min.)
4. Homework: Reading Graphs

Day 5, January 12
Ball-Bounce Function (105 min.)

Day 6, January 17
1. Rod-stamping Function (60 min.)
2. Pendulum Swing Exploration (introduction) (45 min.)

Day 7, January 19
End-of-Quarter Binder Organization and Reflection (105 min.)

Day 8, January 23
1. Peer binder review (30 min.)
2. Pendulum Swing Exploration (75 min.)

Day 9, January 25
1. U-Say, I-Say Game and graphing (60 min.)
2. Functions brainstorming (20 min.)
3. Introduction to Children's Book Challenge

During the next week and a half, students worked in groups on the Children's Book Challenge. We did the View Tube Exploration, and students did a Problem of the Week that involved exploring the Ramp Height versus Distance question. Students presented completed books on Thursday, February 8. Students worked a total of seven days on the Children's Book Challenge.

Unit Plan #2: (Chapter 3: Exploring the Respiratory System)
Carrie Wong

Day 1: Preassessment
Activities: (1) Hold your breath. (2) Freewriting: What makes it possible for you to breathe?
Purpose: Students will understand the need for breathing. Students will reveal what they know about breathing.

Day 2: Engage
Activities: (1) Look at lung tissue (healthy and emphysema).
(2) Freewriting: How did looking at lung tissue with emphysema make you feel?
Purpose: Students will see what happens inside lungs exposed to smoking tobacco. Students will understand that there are consequences for choices we make that affect our health.

Day #3: Explore
Activities: (1) Breathing rate. (2) Measuring lung capacity.
Purpose: Students will learn that people have different breathing rates and lung capacities.

Day #3.5: Explore
Activities: (1) Comparing lung capacity. (2) Breaths and lung capacity. (3) Identifying own variables.
Purpose: Students will start to see how variables may affect breathing and/or lung capacity.

Day 4: Develop (respiratory system)
Activities: (1) Parts of the respiratory system (paper models).
(2) The Great Respiratory System Race.
Purpose: Students will become familiar with the names of parts of the respiratory system. Students will identify and know functions of each part.

Day 5: Develop (air intake and exchange)
Activities: (1) Flow of air (lung model). (2) O_2 and CO_2 Exchange Game
Purpose: Students will see a simulation of how air is taken in and let out from the lungs. Students will understand that oxygen is absorbed by the lungs and that carbon dioxide is sent back out.

Day 6: Develop/Extend (influences on air intake and exchange)
Activities: (1) Smoking Lung in a Bottle. (2) Freewriting: How did the smoking demonstration make you feel? (3) Research functional relationship between smoking and lung capacity. (4) Please Stop Smoking letter/Stop Smoking billboard.
Purpose: Students will observe the effects of smoking just one cigarette and its influences on air intake and exchange. Students will share insights with a family member or friend and the community.

Days 7–8: Extend (other effects on lung capacity)
Activities: (1) Freewriting: Can you name any other possible factors that may influence lung capacity? (2) Individual research on a functional relationship affecting lung capacity.
Purpose: Students will discover other influences affecting lung capacity (positive or negative).

Day 9: Apply
Activity: Design a lesson plan
Purpose: Students show and share what they learned with others.

Unit Plan #3: (Chapter 4: Math Curse Revisited)
Amy Benedicty and Sean Donohoe

Day 1
Introduction: Putting together function journals, overview of unit, Venn Diagram of types of functions; whole class

Day 2
The ink blob: Modeling, discussion, filling in data sheets, then students do exercise, whole class

Day 3 and 4
Function Toys: filling in data sheets; group work

Day 5
Rice in bottles: discussion of slope, "Function Machine" game; group work

Day 6
Booklets: criteria and brainstorms; whole class and group

Day 7
Booklets continued: finish, critique, assign students to revise them; group

Sean's Unit:
Day 1
Introduction: modeling paper clip and magnet experiment; whole class

Day 2–4
Playing with data: paper clip experiment, finding average ranges, making coordinate graphs; group work

Day 5
Discussion: variables and how to make group decisions in a positive way; whole class and group work

Day 6–10
Rice in Bottles and interpreting slope; group work

Day 11–13
Graphing abstract functions, slopes and intercepts; whole class

Day 14–18
Working on functions books

Day 14–15
Getting into math storytelling through fractions problems; whole class and individual

Contributors

Amy Benedicty left AT&T in 1984 to become an educator and spend school vacations with her own children. She has taught mathematics, Italian, language arts, and social studies to urban middle school and secondary school students.

Mike Benway works as a scientist for Behring Diagnostics Inc. (a division of Hoechst AG) in Boston. He became involved with the Urban Scholars Project while studying cellular and molecular biology and biotechnology at UMASS Boston. He can also be heard drumming for BIRDBRAIN on TVT Records.

Betsy Berry has taught high school mathematics for twenty-seven years and is presently a K–12 mathematics facilitator for Maine's Statewide Systemic Initiative and School Administrative District #3 in Unity, Maine.

Marcy Converse has been a K–8 classroom teacher for fifteen years. Her assignments have included junior high language arts, self-contained elementary grades, and, for the last three years, seventh-grade mathematics.

Sean Donohoe has been teaching students ranging from elementary to high school age in the Bay Area since 1974. He also has extensive experience working with community youth groups in outdoor education programs.

Carrie Wong received her teaching credential from San Francisco State University. Currently she teaches math and science at Ben Franklin Middle School in the San Francisco Unified School District.